Semi Serious

SEMI SERIOUS

An Unexpected Journey to a Deeper Faith

Charlotte Stone

WestBow Press
A DIVISION OF THOMAS NELSON

Copyright © 2012 Charlotte Stone

All rights reserved. No part of this book may be used or reproduced by any means, graphic, electronic, or mechanical, including photocopying, recording, taping or by any information storage retrieval system without the written permission of the publisher except in the case of brief quotations embodied in critical articles and reviews.

WestBow Press books may be ordered through booksellers or by contacting:

WestBow Press
A Division of Thomas Nelson
1663 Liberty Drive
Bloomington, IN 47403
www.westbowpress.com
1-(866) 928-1240

Because of the dynamic nature of the Internet, any web addresses or links contained in this book may have changed since publication and may no longer be valid. The views expressed in this work are solely those of the author and do not necessarily reflect the views of the publisher, and the publisher hereby disclaims any responsibility for them.

Any people depicted in stock imagery provided by Thinkstock are models, and such images are being used for illustrative purposes only. Certain stock imagery © Thinkstock.

ISBN: 978-1-4497-7561-2 (e)
ISBN: 978-1-4497-7562-9 (sc)
ISBN: 978-1-4497-7563-6 (hc)

Library of Congress Control Number: 2012921403

Printed in the United States of America

WestBow Press rev. date: 11/21/2012

Dedication

This book is for my Mom, Martha, and in memory of my dad, Charles, who gave me the foundation for life.

Also in memory of Peggy who lifted my spirits and gave me a dream catcher I have hanging in my truck. She didn't get a chance to read the chapter she appears in.

Table of Contents

Foreword		ix
Acknowledgments		xi
Chapter 1	Introduction	1
	Are You Serious?	7
	Farm Girl Hands	8
Chapter 2	Training	11
	On the Way Down and Up	18
Chapter 3	Rookie	19
	Step Out in Faith	24
Chapter 4	Wings of Wildlife	27
	Cruisin' with Hawks and Eagles	34
	Still Learning	37
Chapter 5	Creature Encounters	40
	Deer Insight	45
Chapter 6	Challenges	47
	Stress Less	55
	A Way Out	57
	Top Ten Things Trucking Taught Me about Trucking and about Life	62
Chapter 7	Encouragement	65
	The Song of the Trailer	74
	Praise for the Heavens	76
Chapter 8	The Seasons	80
	Winter Driving Tips	89

	One Shot	91
	The Unnamed Rivers	93
Chapter 9	On the Road with God	94
	View from My Windshield	103
	Remembering History Lived	105
	She Knew Her Name	107
Chapter 10	The Cross Lady	111
	The Big Picture	120
Chapter 11	Real Words	123
	Fear and Trust	133

Foreword

"Hi," she said with a big grin as she extended her hand to me. "My name is Char. I'm off the road until tomorrow morning." The puzzled look on my face served as her cue to clarify. "I drive a truck." An hour and a half later, I locked up the building and we left the church, each heading for the parking area. As I recall, it was a good thing that it was a pleasant Saturday evening. We stood beside our vehicles and I listened for another half hour. Char was definitely a fascinating story-teller and a faith-filled believer.

Semi Serious is the happy marriage of daily divine encounter and the poetic and prayerful outpouring of the spirit as response. As a conscientious observer with a delightful turn of phrase, Char takes what seems to be the simplest occurrence and guides the eyes of the heart to see the complexity and depth of God's interaction with His creation. What a blessing it is to be reminded again to *keep* awake and *stay* aware of *all* that God is doing *for good*.

Enjoy the trip!
Rev. Linda Hansen Bibb

Acknowledgments

God is the author of our faith and as such He often puts other people in our lives to move us closer to the faith He would like us to have. I would like to thank some people who influenced me in my faith journey. The list is undoubtedly incomplete.

Thank you to my childhood friend, Diane, who invited me to the Billy Graham movies. My oldest cousin, Ethel, spoke of spiritual things she had experienced as a nurse. My high school language teacher, Helen, recognized the writer in me and gave me the courage to explore that talent. My church choir director, Maurice, encouraged my singing, though I was so shy I didn't use it well for years. Another high school teacher, Lois, taught me to be honest and open in leadership. A college instructor, Ann, showed me how tough grief can be. One of my principals, Sister Jean, believed in me as a teacher and as a person and gently strengthened me to be better. Pastor Cliff challenged me to write down what I believed on index cards, instead of worrying about my doubts. I have rewritten those index cards each decade, which has helped me see the growth in my faith through people and circumstances in my life. It also gives me perspective as I see my children developing their faith, since my faith is in black and white. Pastor Troy perceived my struggle and gave me some help to work through it. Sister Mary was a wonderful listener and offered a different perspective. To my friend, Jean, who shared both our faith and our young motherhood experiences, I am ever grateful. She continues to be one of my prayer warriors. My cousin, Julie, whose firm faith and prayers are both an encouragement and an example, I am thankful for her willingness to pray for me any time I need it. Living in a small town with my preschool children, I found friends for my children and discovered a kinship with Claudia, who parented in the way I wanted to parent. I also appreciated all the women in Lydia circle and Ruth circle. The Bible studies and discussions went a long way to developing my faith and many are still dear friends. While attending and participating in retreats, many women inspired me as we shared our faith moments. I am grateful to Pastor Linda, who at my request, held me accountable to become more active in my church after recovering from divorce. She welcomed my participation in a disciple class whenever I was able to get home and led me on a journey I didn't know I needed to take.

I would also like to thank those who contributed in big and small ways to the publication of this book. First, there would not be a book if not for my son-in-law, Jason, who planted the idea of a change in career. As a trucker, he was a great support when I was learning the intricacies of trucking. To my children, Lauren and Bob, for the great support they have given me in the sudden urge to write this book. Thanks to Bob's friend, Ashley, who provided yet another pair of eyes on the manuscript. My consultant Maggie, at Westbow, was an invaluable source as I struggled with my first experience in the world of publishing. Soon after the writing was done, my naiveté about the amount of work still left to be done became very clear to me, and throughout the process, her patience was unwavering.

1
Introduction

For I know the plans I have for you, says the Lord, plans for welfare and not for evil, to give you a future and a hope.
—Jeremiah 29:11

It was late that night in May 2005. I struggled to finish my work in the empty middle school classroom. The tension in my mind and body was beginning to sap my ability to form the Individual Education Programs for some students for the next year. I lived thirty minutes from the school and usually worked until I was done before I left for home. Calling my adult daughter and chatting for a bit before resuming the work on my computer would help me cope with the long hours.

This particular evening my son-in-law answered and I voiced some of my frustrations at the workload so late in the year. He listened for a while and then said, "You should try trucking, Momma." His words stopped my line of thinking, because they came out of the blue. Well, not for him, because he was a trucker. For me the thought was so incredible I could hardly take it seriously. Without missing a beat, he continued to talk about the possibility. "You could do it, Momma." Slowly I began posing questions for him. I needed to know how in the world I would learn trucking. Where would I get the training necessary? When could I start? How much would that training cost? How long would it take to become good enough to get a job? What were the job prospects?

At the end of the conversation, he promised to get online and find the answers to my questions. I was skeptical about this new possibility, but told him to go ahead. I hung up and turned toward my desk when a tremendous peace came over me. The tension in my body was gone and my mind relaxed as I enjoyed the serenity. A thought zipped across my mind, *Uh-oh, I think I'm going to be driving a big rig!* As I continued my work, this thought would pop up once in a while. I knew the calm came from God, and I was intrigued at the thought of traveling all over the country.

My son-in-law reported that a highly recommended school was just a half hour from my house. The costs were reasonable and the amount of time indicated I could train in the summer and have a job by the fall. Looking back, it's amazing that such an outrageous career move would hold an appeal for this divorced grandmother whose two kids were out of college and on their own. It all came down to the peace that washed over me that night. This was God's new door opening in my life.

Knowing it was His will was one thing—telling my principal I was going to resign suddenly was another. Shocked that I was leaving, she asked what I was going to do. It still seemed like an extraordinary step to take, so I said, "I'm not ready to talk about that right now." Then she shocked me by asking if I was going to seminary. Working in a public school I didn't talk about my faith much, but apparently it showed. A couple of days later when I finally got up the courage to talk to her, I told her she wouldn't believe it. After hearing my next career, she said it didn't surprise her.

"That's the other side of you—the adventurous side that worked in Yellowstone one summer and recently jumped out of an airplane."

My family had rarely traveled when I was young. Summers were busy on the farm, and my parents felt education was important, so we took only short trips on weekends. When I took German in high school, I learned the word *wanderlust* and knew I had always felt it. So now I enjoy seeing new parts of the country and taking in the sights, sounds, people, and unique characteristics that define them. As an adult, I embraced the wanderlust inside as often as possible without letting it get in the way of my responsibilities. Accepting that part of who God made me and acting on the desire for adventure in small doses throughout adulthood undoubtedly helped me be open to such a drastic life change.

Within two weeks of the unexpected phone conversation with my son-in-law, I had submitted my letter of resignation and told the rest of the faculty about my decision; all without yet applying to the community college training school. Somehow I knew this was what God wanted me to do, and He would help me do it. After the initial shock, my colleagues had many questions. The one I couldn't answer was, "What's your CB handle?" They decided to have a contest to give me suggestions. The winner was TNT, meaning Teacher Now Trucker.

As early as January 2006, I wrote in an e-mail, "I am beginning to realize this time is not about trucking and it's not about the money. I'm keeping an open mind. Several people have mentioned I should write a book. I know that is a remote possibility, but I'm willing to take notes and journal when I can. I'm open to the idea of the book a little more, because the ideas are coming in a different way than I am used to. Normally, I get the first couple of lines or even a whole verse of a poem before I put a pen to paper. My poems are often nameless until completed, as if the title is secondary to the poem. Last week the titles started coming to mind - even the title of the book: *Semi Serious*. It's very strange and I know it'll be a long time coming, but I'm writing them down."

I liked the title immediately because it had special meaning for me. I was serious about learning to drive a semi, even if others had their doubts. After all, I had resigned from teaching. I felt strongly this was what I was supposed to do, and I had no job to fall back on. For example, an instructor teased me about my gloves, "Char doesn't want to break a nail." I was offended at her misunderstanding of who I was; a farm girl whose hands had endured countless scrapes, scratches, dirt, muck, and many broken nails. Ironically I break fewer fingernails when trucking than I did when I was teaching. Her comment motivated me even more. When I interviewed for my first trucking job, the recruiter knew me as the mother of his son's friend, a former pastor's wife, and a teacher. He was kind but found it hard to believe I would make it as a trucker. I mentioned having driven a tractor at age eight. I drove only thirty to forty feet forward and back to help Dad get bales in the hayloft, but it was a beginning. I told him about working in Yellowstone one summer at age fifty-four, including going whitewater rafting. The clincher was that I had gone skydiving at age fifty-six to complete the life list I made in college. He said, "You did that?" and then added, "You just might be adventurous enough to drive a truck."

In other times in my life, I have felt moved to do things that didn't make sense. In those times, I found myself resisting the urge until I realized I was arguing with God. But when submitting to doing something I would never have done on my own, I discovered it was just the thing I or someone else needed. At times, a quiet voice has even spoken words I needed to hear.

I began writing poems, and through the years I have shared a few. Some were better than others, and some took a long time to write. Meanwhile, I waited for an indication it was time to write the whole book, because I knew I wasn't writing it for me: this is God's book, and He is my inspiration in writing and in life. He has shown His love for me through common and extraordinary circumstances as I've rolled along this country's highways.

Praying comes naturally when I spend hours on the road. Whether it's an interstate or a smaller highway, I am out in God's creation. Radio stations come and quickly fade, and in the mountains they all but disappear. CDs pass the time, but are not easy to change, so when I tire of the songs I shut it off. In the silence, communication with God goes both ways. Years ago, I developed a habit of morning devotions. I've learned to pay attention to the thoughts that pop into my mind during that time, so I follow up on them. Maybe someone needs a phone call or a letter of encouragement. One Sunday during morning devotions, I felt an urge to get to church, and in spite of my car not starting, I still went by taxi. I was glad I had forced myself to go, because during that service, I prayed with the congregation as the pastor led us in a prayer that changed something inside me—a change I didn't realize until a couple weeks later when I was completely calm in a situation that ordinarily would have panicked me. The effects of prayer and devotions are just as strong in the cab of my truck before a long day of driving as they were in my favorite recliner before school.

For me, being a Christian has changed over the years, with a variety of commitments and involvements. I've gone from a pew sitter, to very involved, to pastor's wife, and back to just me sitting in the pew again. I needed time to heal, but after several years I began to feel out of touch. Becoming a pew sitter after having been so active felt awful. I then felt the Lord telling me, "The divorce didn't put you in the back pew, Char. You did, and now I need you to get out of that pew and help me again." I talked to my pastor and asked her to help me be accountable, to be more involved. I had to think outside the box a bit, because I was home for only thirty-four hours a week on break. She invited me to participate in a disciple Bible study class whenever I could make it with my unpredictable schedule. She used the word *covenant* in relation to the class, because it was a year's commitment. It was a wonderful, thoughtful, thankful, humbling time of growth for me.

Shortly after that prayer and while taking the class, I began reacting differently to events around me. During a period of weeks, I recalled times in the past I wasn't proud of. I talked to God about them and confessed my part in each memory, and then the memory faded. After two weeks of tears, I was ready to be done with it. I told God I wanted the truth, but then expected the worst, as I pictured Jack Nicholson responding to Tom Cruise in *A Few Good Men*: "You want the truth? You can't handle the truth!" Instead, I was flooded with memories of times I had done something to help someone else, like a letter, a phone call, a visit, or even a hug that was appreciated or made a difference to them—small things to me, but things I realized God had noticed and was reminding me that they were important. It affirmed who I had been and could be again.

I entered trucking with the desire to hold onto the peace that came over me after my son-in-law planted the surprising initial idea. However, I didn't foresee the other divine gifts I would be given along the way. It has been a wonderful experience getting to dwell in God's world, getting to know God so much better, in a different way. I am amazed at how enriching this time has been, and although I am often shy about witnessing, it has been hard to keep it inside. From the on-the-road ministry giving away my daughter's handmade crosses when urged by God to do so, to sharing my testimony in my church, to guest preaching a few times at other churches, to beginning study at the School for Lay Ministry, I have embraced the opportunities God has given me to share my faith. All of these moments of sharing have come from my willingness to let God lead me. I let Him take my hand as I stepped out in faith, not knowing what was on the other side. This book is the culmination of my life-changing experience thus far. Although my trucking adventures are not finished, once again I am following God's nudging and sharing my story.

Dear Lord, thank You for this new direction in my life. Help me learn to do the job well as You would have me do it. You have been with me through many changes in my life, but this is perhaps the most challenging one. I trust You to continue guiding me. In Jesus' name, amen.

Are You Serious?

Stunned silence is first
Then things to think about
Some jokes as they picture it
And in the end their support

Those who know me best
Are aware of my serious side
The part of me who ministers
But can't afford seminary

They also know the side of me
Who longs for adventure
Worked a summer in Yellowstone
And jumped out of a plane

A drastic change in career
Not to be taken lightly
Some still want to know
"Whatever possessed you?"

Throughout the training
Some wondered if I'd make it
But I sacrificed and worked
And was serious about learning

Days I was frustrated
Tired and wanted to give up
But helpful hints at times
Made it easier each day

2006

Farm Girl Hands

Curious hands, touching things
Playing in the grass and dirt
Watching mud ooze out
Through fist-clenching fingers

Hands that climbed trees
So painfully in the spring
Not noticeable in the fall
After calluses acquired

Hands that gripped garden hoe
And pulled unwanted weeds
Hands that felt the scratch
Of prickly radish leaves

Hands that gently milked
Or shoved a stubborn calf
Hands that scratched the ears
And rubbed pig's bristly back

Hands that carried bales of hay
From baler to hayrack to barn
Scratched and pricked with thistles
Dividing each bale for food

Hands scratched by kittens
Barbed-wire fences, rusty nails
Worn-out boards, sharp gravel
And occasional berry bush

Hands that took the scum off
The cattle's watering tank
Hands that rubbed cold water
On bloated belly of lamb

Hands that wielded shovel
Cleaning the filthiest barn
Or hog house and chicken coop
Then fluffing new clean straw

Farm hands out of place in school
Too rough for soft clothing
Forever chapped in cold weather
And hidden on certain occasions

This woman lives in town now
But still has farm girl hands
Hands separating dirt from roots
In digging new flower beds

Going out to check the garden
Means dirt under fingernails
Rubber gloves bought and forgotten
Garden gloves used only sometimes

Feeling the work I'm doing
Tiniest weed, newly sanded wood
Cleanest plate, softest flower
Or well-combed Labrador retriever

When I'm 90, I would guess
I'll still have farm girl hands
Unafraid to touch and explore
And feel and sometimes hurt

1988

2
Training

*Therefore encourage one another and build one
another up, just as you are doing.
—1 Thessalonians 1:11*

After resigning from my teaching position, I applied and was accepted to the training school. I was able to start the classroom part of the training two days a week in the evening before the end of teaching for the school year. There were only three of us in the class, and I found studying from the book quite easy. When summer came, I was anxious to get hands-on experience with trucks and switched to a daytime class. This class was larger, and the students seemed more intent on learning all they could to get a job as soon as possible. I was particularly good at understanding the new rules regarding logbooks, which show the times a driver is sleeping, off duty, driving, or on duty (loading and unloading). On the days we worked on logbooks, I was allowed to circulate around the room, checking the work of the other drivers.

The guys appreciated it, as it took less time than waiting for the one instructor to check each of them, and I didn't judge their errors—something I learned in my first teaching job. In 1968 near Chicago after the Democratic convention descended into riots, we were taught not to *front* students. The black students were in the minority in our high school, and they were on edge. We were not to confront black students especially. We were not to criticize them in front of their peers. A few words quietly spoken in private did more to change a behavior than did a public reprimand. It's a wisdom I used all throughout my teaching career. I also applied it to parenting and my other relationships.

Part of the time at the training school we were in a classroom setting, but we also were able to go out to the lot, where the semi cabs were parked. Pre-trip inspections are the first step, which means learning how to determine if there is anything wrong that might jeopardize a driver's safety. We had to memorize numerous points, starting with walking up to the truck to see if it was tilted to one side (flat tire) and then making a detailed examination of the tires, wheels, brakes, drivetrain, fuel tanks, and all the parts under the hood. We also had to name the part aloud in a particular sequence as we touched it and voice what problems to look for. I had the sequence memorized, but standing by the truck, I was unsure of exactly which part was which. The truck in front of me didn't look quite like the pictures in the book. Some students had more experience, whereas I didn't even know how to open the hood of a semi to look at the engine. My five-foot-four-inch height was dwarfed by the immense machines, and I had to stretch to reach up high to pull the hood open. The instructors helped me until I learned how to handle it. As I stood by the open driver's door, my head wasn't even as high as the seat. Getting in was like climbing a ladder by skipping a step three times. Trucking has done wonders for my calf muscles.

After doing pre-trips until we were sick of the cadence, there came the day when we got behind the wheel and turned the key. The instructor first drove around the short route from the truck lot down to a larger lot and back up, explaining exactly when to shift, where to stop, and when to put it in reverse to back up. I was again out of my comfort zone. My partner didn't show that day, so I drove alone with an instructor. After one trip around the course, he got out. He walked beside my truck for a while and then left me alone to go up the hill and back down. I drove that truck all day. We were not to go any faster than third gear. In a car, third gear is almost the top gear. In a truck with ten to thirteen gears, it's barely moving ten miles per hour. I think I got to third gear—I can't tell you for sure—but the truck was going plenty fast enough for me. We practiced these basic skills of starting, stopping, turning, and straight backing until they became familiar to us.

After bobtail training (just the cab, called the tractor), we had to go through the pre-trip inspection of the trailer. Luckily, it wasn't as long because there were fewer things to inspect. Then we learned how to hook up to a trailer. We use the backing skills we had just been practicing. We would back partway under the trailer, set the brake, and get out to see if the huge pin on the bottom of the trailer (the king pin) was lined up with the opening of the fifth wheel of the truck (the round metal that hooks into the trailer). It is the most important part of hooking up to a trailer. If the trailer is too high, the dollies (legs) have to be wound so the trailer comes down and rests on the fifth wheel. Once the kingpin was positioned correctly, we could back up until it was locked in place.

After raising the legs, it was time to attach the two air lines (the tractor brake and the trailer brake) and the electric line (which runs the lights and signals of the trailer). We drove the same route as we had with the bobtail but with activity in the lower lot. We maneuvered our trucks in and out of several barrels to simulate turns at intersections. Some cones limited how far we could swing out. Another student was in the truck with me who had experience driving trucks in the army. I graciously (rather, nervously) allowed him to go first. Then after one round, we had to switch drivers. When it was my turn to go through the barrels, I wasn't so good. I had watched other trucks go through and took my cues from them. My instructor later said the reason for my difficulty was probably because the two of us had a fifty-three-foot trailer, and most of the other drivers had forty-eight-foot trailers. I gave him a look that communicated my dissatisfaction with that distinction. He recovered, saying it was a measure of the confidence he had in our skills. Later, as my co-driver, got out for a smoke break, he said, "You certainly don't need my help." That encouragement felt great!

Whatever amount of time we had spent practicing in the lot, I didn't feel it had been enough the day they said we were going out on the rural roads to practice shifting to the higher gears. Skill levels among students were already quite different by that time, and I was given an instructor of my own. You can surmise what you like from that statement. He directed

Semi Serious | 13

me to an unfamiliar county road to practice shifting all the way to tenth gear and back down to first. We were on a little-used road, so traffic was not impeded as I slowly gained speed and then began to reduce my speed over and over. My flashers were on the whole time to warn the occasional driver who came upon us. I was getting better, but by the tenth gear, I complained about the steering on the gravel road. It was hard to keep the truck steady at fifty miles per hour, as the wheels had a mind of their own. He just told me to keep going. About lunchtime, we switched places, and he drove us back. Not too long after he reached tenth gear, he acknowledged the steering was too loose for gravel. That gave me a boost of confidence in my ability to discern an unsafe situation, although I was a bit frustrated at not being taken seriously.

The next big step was to drive the semi and trailer on city streets. Since I didn't live in Fort Dodge, I was unfamiliar with the streets. If I had to guess, I'd bet even a Fort Dodge native was unfamiliar with some of the streets we drove on. The townspeople have gotten used to our slow trucks and understand when a student is driving. Turning a vehicle with a trailer seems illogical compared with turning a car. A semi needs thirty feet to make a turn, including the lane it's in and the lane it's going to. It's called off tracking, meaning the trailer's wheels take a shortcut when it follows the tractor around a corner. If you don't factor that in, you can hit something with the trailer. A good turn takes up most of the intersection, which initially seems like a selfish thing to do. But it protects other drivers, cars, property, and your truck. It took me a while to become bold enough to go straight out far enough so the trailer wouldn't take out the stop sign. When my daughter was riding with me in the car, she teased me that I turned my car like her trucker husband by going out to the center of the intersection before turning. Apparently, the instructors had done a good job by making that technique such a habit that I used it in my own vehicle.

Day after day, we drove around town, finding more and more difficult turns to make. The instructors directed us clearly and safely as long as we did just as they said. There were times when I doubted their wisdom. When I was told to move into the other lane on a two-lane street to make a right turn safely, I also had to go all the way into the other lane of the street I was turning onto. Midway into my turn, I saw a car coming but was told to keep going: "They'll wait for you." So I took over the whole street while wanting to apologize to the poor driver of that car. Most of my life I found it easy to be a student, but this education was totally different, and I appreciated the instructors' patience.

For several weeks we learned more and more difficult skills, such as backing into a dock and parking. We first practiced with cones in the big lot. They wanted us to learn how to back up using only our side mirrors—no sticking my head out the window. I finally figured out my brain had trouble reversing a mirror image. Also, the mirror tells me where the trailer is in relation to the tractor, but not in relation to the dock. If the back of the trailer is at an angle to the dock, a forklift driver isn't going to jump a gap from the dock to get in my trailer. When we got better, we were able to practice at docks around town at empty warehouses or stores. Practicing with the real thing made such a difference. One dock we practiced on was by the wall of an empty store with a railing on the other side. Trying to avoid scraping the trailer or tractor was scary. Backing continues to be my weakest skill, but luckily the percentage of time backing is small and the speed is much slower than going forward. We had a safety sign on our mirrors at the training school with the initials, G.O.A.L., which meant Get Out And Look; I still have to use that method sometimes at warehouses I haven't been to before. It reminded me of when I was teaching, we always had to have goals. I was glad I didn't have to make all the required teaching goals any more, although I still set personal goals.

One afternoon, the driving instructor took us to a railroad crossing on a hill and asked us to come to a complete stop. He explained how to start up using the Johnnie Brake, a hand lever that applies the trailer brakes when the left foot is on the clutch and the right foot is on the brake. It is a good skill to know. We were also taught how to parallel park. When I lived in Hyde Park in Chicago in the 1970s, I got pretty good at parallel parking. A friend stopped by our Chicago apartment and complimented my husband on his parallel parking job. He deferred and pointed to me as the one who squeezed into a space that left less than a foot in front and in back. However, parking a seventy-foot semi is quite a different skill. With only cones for reference points, I was never sure how well I did. Backing something with a trailer is the opposite of backing a car. If you want the back of the trailer to go left, you turn the wheel right. If you want it to go right, turn the wheel to the left. Using the skill out on the road, I do well enough, but I've seen many truckers who are better at it.

A number of instructors taught at the school, and we found out each morning who we would be working with. It was good to have a variety, as each one had different ways of teaching and connecting with the students. It reminded me of teaching middle school students, who are all unique individuals and need different methods of encouragement and motivation. Back when I was teaching, the hardest yet most rewarding part was trying to find the exact impediment to learning. Two special education teachers had to help me with one poor reader until we figured out he pronounced the vowels as you would in Spanish. I know that the trucking instructors consulted with one another on how they might best help a student. I also could see other trucking students reacting better to one instructor over another.

Toward the end of the summer, the school was grading us on skills as they saw we had mastered them. After passing all of the school's skills tests, the final step was passing the tests at the DMV. After filling out some paperwork, we waited for them to call us. The knowledge test was taken on a computer, and it took most of the day, because there were so many of us. Another day we brought a semi and had to show our knowledge of the pre-trip inspection. There was lots of waiting that morning as each of us went with an examiner. After I passed my pre-trip exam, I asked one of our instructors, "What would you guess was her most frequent comment?"

He said, "Just relax."

"Yes!" I laughed. "She said it several times." It was the most nervous I've ever been before a test—totally out of my comfort zone.

The field test on turning and backing was done in one afternoon session. We had been taught what the test involved and practiced even with the exact distances of the short route. We had to turn right and get as close to the cone on the corner without touching it, then drive a hundred feet between cones, drive forward out of the cones at a forty-five degree angle, and then back up between the cones again. In practice, I regularly got to within nine inches of the cone on my turn, so my turning skills were good, but I worried about my backing skills. When I seriously flattened the cone on the turn, costing me several points, I was very upset. I also missed a few points on backing, which meant I failed. I couldn't go on to the drive test. Back at the school, they had me run through the short route again. I was totally embarrassed and frustrated with myself. The other students were sympathetic and gave me encouragement for my retry the next day. I rarely failed a test in school, and it was a humbling experience. The following day I went back and passed the turning/backing test. Finally it was time for the drive test. We could miss a total of thirty-five points. I missed only thirteen. Instead of a diploma, the school gave us an official Iowa Central Transportation cap. I treated myself to a special dinner for passing the DMV tests. I splurged on sea scallops, a twice baked potato, fresh asparagus, and chocolate chip mint ice cream. I had my CDL. I was officially a trucker. It felt almost as good as the day of skydiving.

Dear Lord, this is all so strange to me. I sometimes wonder if I'll ever gain the skills to make a living in a semi. You have led me in this direction, and I have to trust You as I continue learning as much as I can. Thank You for being with me in all circumstances. In Your presence, amen.

On the Way Down and Up

When the possibility came along
She asked for some assurance
During her morning prayers
About this impossible dream

Tentative courage grew strong
With the excited response
As she shared with friends
The riskiest of all her dreams

What for years seemed scary
Became the thing to do
It just felt like the right time
To experience an old dream

It was an unbelievable sight
During an awesome flight
Of wonder at the reality of
A 36 year-old dream fulfilled

The trip down from the sky
Has lifted her up and around
A corner without looking back
Except in disbelief at a dream

The pride of accomplishment
Has changed her perspective
On the person she had become
And her dream changed to a gift

2002

3
Rookie

I can do all things through Him who strengthens me.
—Philippians 4:13

With my CDL in my billfold after a successful interview, I was ready for a few days of orientation. The school instructors knew the company well and made sure I understood their policies and forms to use. Several new drivers were learning about this company, but only one of them was someone who trained with me. He had been a successful bull rider in rodeos and decided trucking was a safer option. Before our company would assign us to a truck, we had to go out for three weeks with a trainer on trips with a loaded trailer. The first week I trained with another trainee who had not been a student of my training school. He was in the right lane on a busy four-lane street when the instructor told him to turn right at the light. He pulled straight out, but then turned left. The quiet-spoken instructor said, "What are you doing?" In the afternoon, this driver was asked to make a left turn from a left lane and turned *right*. The instructor yelled, "Are you listening to me?" I was more than nervous with driving errors that were so dangerous to us and the vehicles around us. My daughter agreed and told me not to go on a trip with him. When I got back to the school, I talked to one of the instructors and told him my family did not want me to go out on a long trip with that driver. He agreed with me. Now when I drive, I picture other drivers as someone in my family, a friend, or even a former student of mine. It helps me keep an attitude of protection for all kinds of drivers around me no matter their level of skill or wisdom. For instance, I saw a semi following so close to a car in the left lane that the driver had no way even to see if the middle lane had an opening for her. I braked so she could see I was giving her a big space for her to escape a dangerous driver. She recognized my move and came over and waved out her window in appreciation.

My first week in training was with an instructor who was good-natured, and I even told the other trainee coming with us that she would enjoy the week. It turned out my expectations were wrong, as the instructor was not himself for some reason. Some of the things he suggested we do were unsafe according to the standards set by the school he taught at, and I ended up apologizing to the other woman. My concern was at such a level that I talked to the director of the school about it.

Only flatbed trips were left when the instructor advised me of my next week's training run. He told me, "You don't have to do any of the work of tarping the load and securing it. You would just do half the driving." Well, it was August, and after watching the trainee and instructor getting dirty and sweaty with the work of tarping, I found ways to help them. They appreciated that I got the wide straps and the winches out of the storage area and placed them on the ground at appropriate intervals. They even taught me how to use them. They would then follow me and tighten the straps and winches further. It was a good week, and I had an opportunity to have a positive conversation with the trainee.

The trainer for my third week had been in the truck with me only one time—when I was driving in town. The other student with us had been talking to him about women they saw on our route. Because I didn't know the instructor, I didn't object to the demeaning conversation. At one point he knocked on his window with his knuckles and then sharply said, "Watch out for your trailer wheels! You're hitting the curb with them!"

Somewhat chagrined, I replied, "I didn't notice."

"Well, I was knocking on the window."

"Was that for me? I thought you'd seen another woman to talk about."

When I found out I had to go out with those same two men, I wasn't looking forward to that week. I did my best to be alert to everything I was doing, but as I was leaving a toll booth in the dark near Chicago, I had trouble getting into first gear. I said, "I don't know why I get so nervous."

His crusty reply was, "What are you going to do about it? It's up to you." Pause. "I guess it depends on how badly you want to be a truck driver." The truck was moving by then, but I didn't feel like answering. "Have you hit anything?"

"No."

"Have you run over anyone?"

"No."

"Have you had an accident?"

"No."

"Are you a good driver?"

"Yes."

"Are you a safe driver?"

"Yes."

"Then what are you worried about?" I was beginning to feel as though I were in the Marines hearing a sergeant get in my face. But then he said, "I'd sleep in the bunk behind either one of you. And I can't always say that about students." There it was— a compliment! I suddenly felt like a trucker. It was a great feeling. *I can do this.*

With the three weeks of training over, we were officially hired and were told to bring enough things to last us a week. The company didn't have enough trucks in town, so four of us carpooled down to Kansas, where they had another terminal. I was getting a cold and spent a good deal of time in the back seat trying not to cough and spread germs. Two of us were dropped off in McPherson, Kansas, and the other two left for Oklahoma. The shop and office were closed, and it took a while to find the keys to my truck. A driver drove in, helped us find empty trailers, and directed us to the shipper. With a couple prayers, I found the courage to take that first trip alone. I managed to remember enough of my training to get the load and find my way down the road to the receiver. Our training school's goal was to teach us the correct way to do things to keep us safe during the first year, and after that we could call ourselves *truckers*. I was on my way.

A few times of my rookie year were embarrassing, difficult, and

Semi Serious | 21

sometimes scary. I frequently forgot to open the trailer doors before I backed into the dock. Warehouse people greeted this error in a variety of ways: "It would be easier to unload you if I could get my forklift into the trailer." Whether they were gracious or rude, I was red-faced. After making the same mistake again and again, I gave up and just joked along with them.

The most difficult part of my rookie year was how to deal with a missed turn. Finding a place big enough to turn a seventy-foot vehicle around is not easy. Going around the block is rarely a good idea unless you can find large enough streets. I remember going into a dark parking lot of a large store in a town I'd never been in, but it was the easiest place because the store was closed and the lot was big enough. As I was getting turned around, I saw some boys on their bikes coming into the lot. I couldn't tell how old they were or why they were biking after dark with no lights, so I was a bit nervous. I stopped my truck so they could go on without worrying about my semi. Then one boy pumped his fist for the air horn. I thought, *Why not?* I sounded the horn in the empty lot, and they all loved it and waved their appreciation. I may have been imaging it, but their biking seemed to have more energy as they went on their way. When they were out of sight, I finished turning around as I realized anyone who drives a big rig is respected by a variety of people. It reminded me of when I was in the process of sliding my tandems (moving the trailer wheels so the weight of the load is balanced on all axles), when workers from a small warehouse across the street were just getting off work. A young man stopped in his tracks and asked, "Do you drive that thing?" When I said yes, he said, "All by yourself?" He was so incredulous, I had to laugh. "How in the world can a little woman like you drive that big thing?" His response was so spontaneous and genuine; it went a long way to help me forget rookie mistakes I'd been making. In his eyes I was a trucker—period.

Winter was filled with scary times that first year. Growing up in Minnesota helped me some, but weather doesn't play favorites. Though I was not forced to drive in a snowstorm, I couldn't wait for it to melt and still get any driving done. Sometimes there's no place to stop when the flakes hit the windshield. During one storm, I got off in Bloomington, Illinois, when it was getting dark and the flakes were getting bigger. The next morning I woke up to several inches of snow causing havoc in the truck stop parking lot. A call to dispatch let them know I needed to wait because it wasn't safe to leave. By afternoon, many of the trucks were leaving, and I decided the plows must have the roads taken care of. It was okay until I got near Peoria. Perhaps a snow plow driver overslept or maybe it was an area that got more than the usual amount of snow, but it was slow going. Soon I realized when I was out on the highway that I would not be able to get off the interstate for a long time. In single file, we weaved among semis, SUVs, pickups, and cars that were stuck on a shoulder, in a lane, or in the median. By the time I got on the road, the plows just went straight past the ramps, building a ridge to discourage anyone from trying to exit. The tow trucks were beginning to remove vehicles from the exit ramps by starting at the bottom. It was a tense trip, and I was thankful I had a heavy load of huge rolls of paper, which kept my vehicle in close contact with the road in spite of the slippery snow pack.

Within the first year, I heard that the rookie who was such an admirer of women rolled his semi on a ramp in dry weather. There's only one way to do that—speeding—and there is only one result—losing your job. He wasn't hurt, but it was a sobering reminder of how quickly life can change in the world of big machines. I am not ashamed to say that many times my prayers have not been enough to assuage my fears, whether navigating a snowstorm, driving into a city I don't know, or feeling unsafe parking on the street until a warehouse opens its gate. Those are the times I have called some good friends to ask for prayers, and they were always willing. Thank you, friends!

Lord, thank You for my safety yesterday. Help me be alert to hazards on the road today. Above all, Lord, give me the wisdom to keep the people around me safe. In Your care, amen.

Step Out in Faith

Step out in faith
Without a clue
To a future
Only God knows

Step out in faith
To what God wants
What He may do for me
What I may do for Him

Step out in faith
Go deep in prayer
With listening ears
To hear Him whisper

Step out in faith
Ask and receive
Wisdom, strength
Courage, and love

Step out in faith
To an unknown
A new way of life
In the care of God

Step out in faith
Hand in His hand
His heart in mine
My life for Him

Step out in faith
Follow His lead
Trust Him always
For He knows best

Step out in faith
Do not be swayed
In Him alone
My future depends

2005

"God's artistry"
God can even make a sculpture of perfection
in the midst of a snowstorm.

4
Wings of Wildlife

> Look at the birds of the air: they neither sow nor reap nor
> gather into barns, and yet your heavenly Father feeds them.
> —Matthew 6:26

Besides being a farmer, my father loved nature and referred to God as the Creator, perhaps because he was so close to creation in his work and in his avocation of ornithology. He called himself a birder, but many people would say he went far beyond that. He could identify almost as many birds by their songs as he could by sight. He had loved birds since he was a boy and was especially active in protecting those whose numbers were dwindling. He thought hawks in particular were misunderstood and even left ten acres of woods on his farm as a refuge for both birds and animals. Dad loved birding so much he wrote a book on it, *Birding From a Tractor Seat*, but I never thought I'd find myself birding from a (semi) tractor seat. I was as near-sighted as my father was far-sighted, so I was never able to identify clearly the birds he pointed out to me, but I loved going on the birding trips he organized. He was patient with me, because he understood I couldn't see as well as he could. He told us about when he was a boy, his parents had asked the eye doctor to check his brother's eyes. In those days, the eye doctor traveled to his patients with a black bag full of glasses of varying lenses. Dad was on the farmhouse porch when the doctor asked his brother what kind of animal was standing by the barn. Dad thought it was a ridiculous question because he could see the flies on the back of the horse. He was shocked when his brother said it was a cow! He understood at that young age his eyesight was unusual.

Dad's favorite resident in the woods was a red-tailed hawk. He would playfully point to a mouse or gopher that ran from his tractor, and the hawk was soon there for dinner. Dad knew the hawk didn't really need his help, but it was fun. Now as I drive down the road and see hawks sitting on signs and fence posts or diving with talons open to snag lunch, I can see the rusty tail and my thoughts go to my dad. He would be pleased to see how plentiful hawks and other rare birds have become. One day on the open road, a coyote came up out of the grass in the ditch and ran in front of my semi. I saw movement just in time to brake and missed him. As I sighed in relief, a red-tailed hawk swooped down in front of my truck. I had no time to react, but as he safely soared away, it was almost as though my dad were saying, "Good job missing that coyote." Dad has been gone almost twenty years, but seeing the number of unmolested hawks reminds me of the work he did to protect them.

I remember another quick sighting of his favorite hawk driving in northern Missouri on I-29 toward Iowa. There was a narrow band of snow going through Nebraska and southern Iowa, and when I got to the area, I was grateful to see the highway was just wet and the only snow was on the grass. Just then, a red-tailed hawk swooped down into the right ditch and, without landing, made a perfect left-handed grab for lunch and flew off. I've seen that same move many times, but this time I could see his lunch against the white background of the snow. It was like watching an athlete make a great move, and I was thankful the snow allowed me to see his successful catch.

On a clear spring day near Waverly, Iowa, I saw white objects on a small lake up ahead. It was very windy, but they didn't look like whitecaps. Coming closer, they looked like birds, but were too big to be gulls and too many to be swans. As I came close to the lake, I did a double take when I realized I was looking at dozens of pelicans. In Iowa? On a small lake? I'd seen them before on a much larger lake, but I was astounded to see them in rural Iowa. Seeing birds so far out of their habitat made me think they were a little like me out here in the freedom of the road, so far from the life in a classroom I had known for years.

Toward the end of a fall trip I was close to home near Fort Dodge, Iowa, when I saw a small family of swans fly overhead in front of my truck. They were aiming for their favorite pond, where I had seen them sitting in the water many times and had watched the young ones grow up, but I had never seen them in flight. Their black beaks were a stark contrast to their white plumage. Their necks seemed to stretch out forever and were so different from the graceful curve seen when they rested, but what a treat to see them fly!

On another occasion, I was going to a shipper down on a dead-end street in Chicago, with warehouses on the right and a wall on my left, separating the street from the I-294 toll road. Just to my left on a six-foot wide strip of grass, I spotted a pair of Canadian geese followed by five yellow, fluffy goslings. The parents gave me the eye as I drove by to be sure I kept my distance from their toddling offspring. It was awesome to see the family adjusting to a life in a busy metropolitan city.

One year, about the time when birds flock south, I passed a field with a few spots of white amid the dark. Something didn't look right, because crops were long ago harvested. Then the mystery was solved as I came closer and saw the field literally covered with Canadian geese, with a few white gulls in amongst them. There must have been at least a thousand of them. The field held few empty spaces as they rested during migration. Some people view these geese as a nuisance, but I am old enough to remember when they were rare, and now they are plentiful: "The meadows clothe themselves with flocks" Ps. 65:13a. I found this verse to be very fitting for the situation, even if I'm pretty sure the Bible was referring to sheep.

Several times I have had to brake to avoid birds that were not making good use of their wings. For instance, a gaggle of young geese did a fast walk across the interstate. The car beside me in the left lane braked and missed them. Nine or ten of them were in the road, and I had no option but to slow down and continue straight because of heavy traffic. Just before I got to the last goose on the ground, it flew up out of the way. I'm not sure if it was by its own power or the force of the air the truck was pushing in front of it, but I was glad I missed it. In the twilight one night in Kansas, I barely avoided what seemed to be a convention of pheasants. Some were flying as high as my windshield, some were running across the road, and a small flock of fledglings were being herded across the road by their moms. As I tried to account for all of them, I noted they all made it safely across. On a little-used highway in Nebraska, I saw four huge birds crossing the road up ahead. I slowed because they were sauntering. Finally, the wild turkeys realized I was getting close and scooted faster to get off the road and into the woods. Sometimes I wonder how nature's creatures manage to survive with all our vehicles that seem to be built for speed rather than leisure travel.

Once in a while I come across a rare sight as I drive on this country's smaller roads. What I first thought was a black garbage bag full of air caught on a fence was actually a turkey. On a second glance, I saw the male wild turkey in full mating behavior. His tail feathers were spread and standing straight up as he proudly displayed his puffed-up body and slowly strutted. I didn't see the girl he was trying to impress, but I am certain she was there. I often wish I could just stop and take in the whole action going on beside the roadway, but this is also my occupation, my livelihood, and my responsibility, so I have to move on and keep the scenes and actions only in my memory from these times on the road.

I was visiting Mom on the farm for an overnight stay when my brother directed my attention to some wild turkeys in the farmyard late one summer afternoon. We counted three adult hen turkeys and nine young ones. They came toward the house through the open gate and proceeded along Mom's driveway. One adult lagged behind, which made us notice a tenth youngster having trouble finding the opening in the fence. He finally found it and had to walk faster to catch up to his mom, who moved on after he found his way. We kept moving from room to room as they traveled past the house, being careful to stay well back from the windows because the wild birds are so alert to our movement. The group stretched out in a long line as the birds meandered down the driveway toward the road. The leading adult paused at the end of the drive, and we watched a car go by. Then she crossed the road and the rest followed. It seemed to take forever for all thirteen birds to get across safely. A few seconds later, another car came by as the group disappeared into the tall grass of the ditch. It was several minutes before my brother spotted them in the neighbor's alfalfa field. He first saw one of the adults, and we looked more closely, just barely seeing the young. It was so fun to see such a large group of elusively wild birds so close and for such an extended amount of time. I wouldn't have had time to see the whole of that mini journey when I was in my truck.

Mom often sees wildlife in her farmyard that we never saw when I was young. Besides the turkeys, deer often come into the yard as well as all the birds attracted to the various feeders my brother keeps supplied. Perhaps when we were young, the four of us kids running in and out of the house and the other farm buildings made enough racket that the wildlife stayed away.

With the birding background, the love of nature, and the fearlessness of big machines, it's easy to see my father's influence in this book. However, the independent nature of birds, their ability to soar freely as they coast on a breeze, and the determination you see as they flap wings strenuously into a strong headwind remind me of my mother. Much like the headwind, she has known her trials. She was hospitalized in 2006, then went to a nursing home, overcame her weakness, and returned to her home. She had spent sixty years out of the hospital (the last time was when I was born) and had a hard time being caged like a bird. But I could tell her spirit soared upon her return to the farm as I heard her list all the things she could still do. She may not fly as high as she once did, but in January 2012 she turned ninety-eight, and her wings are still beating.

Sitting at a booth in a little café in Wisconsin, I was enjoying my favorite childhood Saturday breakfast of scrambled eggs, toast, and a glass of milk, when I overheard four guys talking a couple tables away. Their conversation was rather loud as they related the close calls they'd had with turkeys and deer. One said, "Who knew turkeys could fly? If I hadn't ducked down below my windshield, he'd have gotten me!" I smiled to think of him ducking inside his truck, but then realized they were talking about being on a motorcycle. One of them talked about an accident he'd heard about, where a deer had tried to leap over a group of motorcyclists and knocked one man right off his bike, killing him. It really gave me pause to realize how dangerous it could be spending sixty-six hours on the road a week, and I was thankful for how protected I am in the truck.

Crossing a two-lane bridge over the Mississippi going into Minnesota, I saw thirty to thirty-five white birds in the backwaters. I recognized them as white egrets, a bird I didn't expect to see in such abundance. They were standing proudly or moving gracefully, almost regally, through the shallow water. If an elite category of bird existed, I would put the egrets, herons, and flamingoes at the top of the list. I know Dad would be happy to see his beloved birds making a comeback.

In Wisconsin, in 2009, I noticed a tall object out in a field near a grove of trees. A second look seemed to indicate it was a bird, but it was so huge! It had to be four feet tall. About the time I began to doubt the reality of it, it stretched taller and flapped its wings. It seemed unreal to come across a bird so rare without being on an intentional birding trip. Driving on down the road, I tried to jog my memory of all the information about birds I acquired living with my dad. The first thing I did when I got home was find my bird guide book to look up whooping crane, but I'd forgotten they're white. It was most likely an adolescent Sandhill crane because of the brown color and the range they were usually seen in across the United States, which included a small area of Wisconsin. A year later while driving in Wisconsin, I heard on the radio someone mention the possibility of being able to hunt Sandhill cranes in their county. It affirmed that my identification of the bird was correct, but I was sad at the thought of such a magnificent bird being shot. Other than an ostrich or emu I've seen in zoos, it was the largest bird I'd ever seen and certainly something I didn't expect to see standing out in a farmer's field in the upper Midwest.

But by far, my favorite bird is our national bird, the bald eagle. They are so distinct by their size, their startling white heads and tails, and also by the slow powerful beat of their wings in flight. One day after all the leaves were gone, I was driving in Iowa toward the Maquoketa River. Against the dark background of the trees along the bank, I saw the white head and tail of an eagle, looking for a fish lunch perhaps. I had time to watch his flight as he crossed in front of me and went on up the river.

I've seen eagles many times in most aspects of their daily lives: soaring along a river looking for fish, perched in anticipation of a meal on a log in a pond, swooping down to grab a small rodent or fish in their talons, high up on the tallest bare branch of a tree, and sometimes just soaring in circles with others as they ride the thermal air currents. Once as I was crossing the Mississippi, I spotted a large bird. The slow beat of its wings, led me to guess it was an eagle, but he was too far away to confirm it. He banked into a turn and came toward me, almost as if he wanted me to see his white head and white tail, so majestic in flight. I was so excited to be right and felt truly ornithological. I'm still thrilled each time I see an eagle.

None of those sightings compared with what I saw toward the end of 645 weary miles on two-lane roads across northern Michigan, Wisconsin, and Minnesota. In September 2011, I was close to the receiver in northern Minnesota and came upon several large birds feeding on the shoulder. They were too big to be crows, so maybe they were vultures. Then a couple birds took off and I saw a bright white head of the one coming my way and a bright white tail of one headed the other way. *Eagles!* Then more of the birds took off, and because of their size, eagles seemed to be everywhere as they tried to gain altitude in the small space between the pine trees and a huge truck bearing down on them, but I counted only three in the second flight. Two gluttons didn't want to leave the feast. By the time they took off, there was only one way to go, and I found myself chasing the last two eagles down the highway, which was at once incongruous being among them and a shame to be scaring such beautiful specimens. I don't usually have to slow up for birds, but it was such an awesome moment I realized I must have slowed down. Seven eagles on one freshly killed deer! I'd never seen more than one at a time and had never seen them on such big prey. It was like some nature painting, but it was so intense it's hard to describe to anyone, as words hardly capture the experience adequately. The scene played in my mind again as if it were in slow motion. I forgot the weariness I had been feeling and thanked God for a chance to see His wonderful wild winged creatures so close.

Dear Lord, thank You for all the ways You have allowed me to see the world of birds the way my father must have been able to see them. The view out my windshield is up where the birds fly; each sighting is a gift from you. Thank You, too, for the example my mother set for me as a woman of strength and courage in her life on the same farm for over seventy-five years. I am Your child, amen.

Semi Serious | 33

Cruisin' with Hawks and Eagles

It was the numerous hawks I noticed first
Hard to believe there were so many of them
My father was a defender of those birds
Back when guns were used before knowledge

As a child, I went birding with Dad, but
With my poor eyesight they looked alike
He knew all the different kinds of hawks
And what to look for to tell them apart

My dad enjoyed the red-tailed in our woods
He pointed as the hawk dived for mice
Running in the freshly turned dirt
Dad and the hawk shared keen eyesight

Now from high up I can enjoy them
My big rig makes up for my sight
As I see a hawk turn toward me
His rusty tail shows on the way by

On fence posts, poles and road signs
Ignoring my rig and the traffic
They sit most often perched solo
Maybe looking for something to eat

One day I passed by two of them
A rusty red tail confirmed the male
They sat with their backs facing me
The other's size/shape made it female

Charlotte Stone

It shocked me to see two together
Red-tailed hawks remind me of Dad
To see the female reminded me of Mom
Dad's gone; one day Mom will join him

But of all the birds I share the skies with
It's the American bald eagle that thrills me
I'm sure I missed some without knowing
Until one banked on a turn toward me

With a view of his back in full glide
I saw the white tail and great white head
I realized I saw him with the same clarity
As Dad could with his far-sighted vision

I'm closer to understanding Dad's passion
Why he worked so hard to protect them
I wish he could see the difference he made
In increased numbers of our national bird

Crossing the Mississippi one winter day
A large bird flew with a slow beat of wings
When it came close, I saw the white head
And was excited to identify it from afar

I've seen more in four years than all my life
Some were just riding the wind currents
Some were eating or looking for food, and
Always the slow, powerful beat of wings

Semi Serious

The best bald eagle picture in my mind
Was the one flying up the Maquoketa River
His head and tail a contrast to the dark trees
A vision not imagined in my childhood

                                    2009

Still Learning

Mom feared lightning
Until the cows got out
In the midst of frustration
Lightning took second place
I learned courage to face fear
To not be afraid of adventure

Mom learned to drive
By practicing her driving
Many her age never did
And she taxied them around
I learned skills developed
Could lead to independence

Mom is personally disciplined
Coming of age in the Depression
Every penny was thinner
Having gone through her hand
I learned material things
Are not so important in life

Mom was attentive to details
Wording minutes just right
Helping us with 4-H, homework
And Sunday school lessons
I learned details matter
And can make life easier

Mom never stopped moving
Whether in house, barn, or field
Her energy was daunting

At eighty I finally caught up
I learned I'm *Mary*, she's *Martha*
And the difference is okay

Mom multitasked before the word
Cooking for a harvest crew
Cleaning, plucking a chicken
Active in community activities
I learned to be thankful
For the conveniences I have

Mom sought to do right
At times she seemed limited
As gray areas came into my life
But she maintained her view
I learned wrong and right
Do not change with time

Mom always tries to be fair
Whether it was food servings
When we were younger
Or gifts of money as adults
I learned she was trustworthy
And became generous myself

Mom was an appreciator
She asks us to do things
But comes to see our work
Complimenting what we've done
I learned it is a rare gift
That I hope to emulate

Mom's favorite verse, Phil. 4:6
"Have no anxiety about anything…"
Gave her strength to stay on the farm
It gives her peace at ninety-four
I learned faith is action
Whether or not it is spoken

2008

5
Creature Encounters

> Oh Lord, how manifold are thy works! In wisdom hast
> thou made them all; the earth is full of thy creatures.
> —Psalm 104:24

A rabbit ran halfway across the road and sat in the left turn area. Another semi was approaching from the opposite direction, and it appeared we would both arrive at *rabbit zero* at the same time. The distance was shorter if he ran back in front of the other semi. However, at the last minute, he decided to take a chance on me. I am not supposed to swerve even for a large animal, so I slowed up some. His timing was bad, but he realized it, and the last four feet he kicked into overdrive. His legs were almost a blur as he safely reached the side of the road and hopefully became wiser.

Not too long after that, I saw a turtle. He was moving pretty good—for a turtle. He looked a bit like a Nazi soldier with his little legs kicking out with every step. Though I missed him, two cars and a semi were behind me. His fate is unknown, but I like to think he decided to pause in the middle before finishing his journey. Driving through Iowa in 2008, when much of the state was under water, I saw two snapping turtles. Their habitat might have been flooded to cause them to come up onto the road. The second turtle had two men beside it. It was hard for me to tell as I passed by if they were trying to help it off the road out of danger or had turtle soup in mind.

In 2006, I got my first good look at a coyote, which made me decide the animal that ran in front of my truck one dark night in Iowa south of Omaha was *not* a coyote. It was too big, had a much longer tail, and was too yellow to be a coyote. I don't know how I missed him. He was there and gone before my foot came off the throttle—just a streak of yellowish fur about the length of the hood. A good guess would be mountain lion or cougar. A news story on the radio said some had been sighted in southern Iowa.

Another animal I saw up close was a badger. He's a so-called lesser animal—unless you're from Wisconsin. He's not commonly admired, but I saw him running in the ditch and was struck by how flat he was across the back. Also, his hair rippled and flowed as he sped along. He was beautiful.

It isn't always wild animals that tug at my heart. A newborn calf in March was quietly standing close to its mother, focused on staying upright. In another pen just beyond them, a farmer was standing in the midst of some other beef cows. He seemed to be studying them. My dad usually knew when a cow was due to calve, and I believe the farmer was watching for some indications of which cow would be the next to deliver.

Passing by a herd of Angus steers on a warm, sunny day in December, I saw three of them running toward the rest of the herd. It may have been feeding time. There were other steers behind them slowly walking in the same direction. All of them moved in a single file, as cows often do. *Steer* and *frolic* are two words I wouldn't put together often, but I witnessed it as a child with our milk cows. In the cold Minnesota winters, Dad kept the cows in the barn all winter. When he let them out in the spring, I loved to watch them literally kick up their heels in the freedom and warmth of the outdoors.

Passing by a farm, I saw some calves chasing a cat in their pen. The cat didn't seem perturbed but kept just far enough in front of them. We had a cat that did the same thing when my kids were little. As they moved faster, the cat moved faster, tantalizing them with how close they came to her.

There is a farm on US 30 in Nebraska with a few pigs the farmer raised outside. Every time I go by, I smile at the memory of one pig that came tearing down the hill in the pen and tried to get others to join in. When they didn't, he ran back up the hill full of energy. Pigs frolic too.

Once on my way to Crete, Nebraska, on a small two-lane highway, I came upon a half dozen Angus steers toying with the idea of coming onto the highway. They were in a farm driveway, and I suspect they had escaped their pasture. I started sounding my air horn while I slowed up. A couple cars were coming from the other direction and slowed down also. The cows were three times larger than a deer, and I didn't want to hit any of them. They finally decided my truck was too big to challenge and scampered back up the driveway. Having grown up with cows, I wasn't sure they would make the good decision. As a teen, I helped a neighbor round up an elusive herd of cows in a cornfield. We could hear those big animals, but we couldn't see them.

Following a pickup in Missouri, I thought I saw debris about to fly out of the bed again and again, but it never did. As I got closer, I discovered a canine passenger in the back barking furiously at every semi they met. Cars merited a casual bark. It was an enjoyable diversion for four miles before the pickup turned into a driveway. The dog was looking toward home, but turned as he heard me pass by. For a second before he was out of sight, he looked at me, quite confused—no barking. I guess he hadn't realized the dreaded semi was right behind him.

Back to the wild in nature, near Fort Dodge, Iowa, an animal I didn't recognize crossed in front of me. It had a funny loping run, almost like an inch worm. I looked at the habitat on either side of the road and knew it liked wetlands. I had just heard a naturalist on Iowa Public Radio talking about the four water mammals found in Iowa: beaver, otter, mink, and muskrat. I eliminated mink and muskrat as too small, and it wasn't a beaver. That meant it was an otter. The only otters I'd ever seen were in Yellowstone Park very early one morning when I was going to catch a snapshot of a sunrise over the lake. A family of otters was fishing for breakfast, and they were fast, graceful swimmers. As they brought their catch to the surface, they lay back in the water with the fish in their paws and ate like hungry truckers. A trip to the library confirmed the animal I saw was an otter.

Though I love seeing deer, I also need to be wary of them. They can do a lot of damage to my truck and themselves if they get in the road. Two of them were on I-80 in Iowa one moonless night. The first one made it to the left lane, and I watched the second one barely make it safely. Just then, the first one panicked and turned back. I barely clipped her, but one headlight immediately faced downward under the hood. I couldn't tell in the dark, but I hoped she wasn't hurt badly. My company wanted to fix the headlight, so I pulled into a truck stop, bought a roll of duct tape, and enlisted the help of two truckers. Even then, it took a while to get the temporary fix done in the dark. God bless those who give a helping hand to their fellow truckers. The next day after I parked the truck in my company lot, I opened the hood to do a post trip inspection and saw an unmistakable piece of pink tongue. The sobs came suddenly as I realized that though I had not killed her outright, the deer was doomed to die of starvation with such an injury to her mouth.

In May 2008, I was on a two-lane road following a smaller truck. I hadn't seen deer yet that spring and figured the females were giving birth and keeping close to their babies in the woods. A deer in the right ditch didn't flinch as the smaller truck went by. She almost looked like a lawn ornament. As I slowed down, her ears started twitching as she was alerted by the change in the engine noise. She turned tail and ran into the woods. She alerted me, too, as I saw four more deer in the next five miles. When I got onto an interstate, I relaxed until I spotted a deer or two in the green grass on the right. They looked as though they were trying to decide which way to go, but I encouraged the appropriate action by sounding my air horn. Thankfully, they turned, flashed their white tails, and disappeared into the woods.

Later, I was behind another truck that had been going the speed limit, when he slowed down to a crawl. Maybe he was turning, but no, he passed the intersection. Finally, a buck scampered into the left ditch, but before we could speed up, he came back on the road and crossed in front of the same truck. He ended up standing by a row of trees near a farmstead. It seemed to be unusual behavior, until I remembered it was hunting season. In the winter of 2009, coming down a long hill near Ida Grove, Iowa, I saw two deer bounding through a snow-covered field. We were on a collision course, so I slowed down as I enjoyed watching them. The first one skidded to a halt. The second one almost ran into the first, but also stopped. They both stood and watched as I went by. What fun!

I'm pretty used to road kill, but the sight of a small fawn tugged at my heart and caused me to wonder how a doe gets her offspring across a highway. Had this mother seen it happen? Could she have prevented it? A couple days later, on a foggy morning, I got my answer. There was a deer in my lane as I was slowing down approaching a town. She stood awhile and then turned to look behind her, but I couldn't see what she was looking at. Then the little one came scrambling up out of the ditch with its out-of-proportion legs somewhat wobbly. The mother walked to the other side of the road and the fawn eagerly followed, more sure-footed on the smooth paving. As I came close, the mother jumped a fence; I worried, but the little creature kept kicking and somehow got over or through it. As I passed, I could see them both clearly—the fawn was still very spotted and from the back looked like mostly hocks. The stress of driving in dense fog for two hours was gone as I witnessed a mother's courage and the youngster's safety.

Once when I was driving north in my car, I saw a deer in the right ditch facing south, but her head was turned back to the north—not typical so close to the road. It was one of the few dry ditches in Iowa that summer. As I passed by, I saw the smallest of fawns by her side. Its head was stretched up to nurse. It was so tiny! I wondered if the doe had accidentally given birth in the ditch. On another day, in spring, my daughter and I were harvesting asparagus along a rural gravel road. Her two young daughters were *helping*. Someone spotted a rabbit, but then just beyond it we saw a deer cross the road, followed by a fawn. The girls didn't look in time to see the deer, but then as the doe and fawn reached the field, they came past us and the kids were able to see the mother trotting and the fawn desperately running to keep up. It was fun to give the girls their first sight of a wild youngster.

Lord, You know how much I have loved animals all my life. Thank You for this career that has given me the chance to see them often as I travel through their habitats. Thank You for the times I have missed injuring them, and forgive me for those few times when I have hit one of them. Help me continue to scan the ditches as I drive. With love for Your creatures, amen.

Deer Insight

Predawn light wakens them
Moving from a resting place
In late winter blending in
Their coats the color of grass
That hasn't awakened anew

Grazing on a roadside hill
They are near and unseen
Until I discern a change
In texture of the grass
A deer appears as magic

Sometimes a solitary one
Or maybe half a dozen
Amazingly hidden in grass
The same tawny color
Challenging to see them

Even in broad daylight
When I am not rushed
The back all that's visible
Causes another look
Till legs and head take shape

After a long season of snow
They are moving to eat
And fend off their hunger
I love to see them quiet
Not running across my path

I saw my first deer
When in my teens
I perched on a tractor
While doe walked unafraid
With twin fawns behind

What excitement it brought
Inspired me to write
One of my first poems
The secret in our woods
Finally revealed to me

Now from the windows
Of this new occupation
I want them to be afraid
To stay far enough away
But close enough to enjoy

But each time I see them
It's still a thrill inside
What a privilege I feel
To experience it often
I savor each sighting

2008

6
Challenges

Have no anxiety about anything, but in everything by prayer and supplication with thanksgiving let your requests be made known to God.
—Philippians 4:6

Challenges in trucking continue to crop up even after six and a half years of experience. A variety of people in the companies I've worked for have helped me with problems, but sometimes I have to figure out the solutions myself or get help from another trucker. Having a mechanical mind helps in problem solving. And even if the company ends up calling a repair professional, he or she will at least have a good idea what the problem is from my description. I try to learn from each situation so I know what can be done to avoid it in the future. Many people help by praying for me regularly and at times I ask for specific prayers. It would be difficult for me to do this job without reliance on God.

As I was slowly driving through a town on highway 22 in Missouri, I was going straight ahead, but found myself at a blind T-intersection. It hadn't been obvious that the street didn't continue past the traffic light until I got to the top of the rise and the street suddenly ended. To my left was a bridge with a weight limit I exceeded. To the right, a sign said, "No right turn." Neither sign said anything about highway 22. Turning on my flashers, I tried to control the rising panic inside, because there were several cars starting to line up behind me. Relieved to see red and blue flashing lights off my left rear bumper, I hoped the officer could clear up my confusion. My first question was, "What happened to highway 22?" It was off to the right on the other side of the cement divider my truck was near. The patrolman was sympathetic to my error and asked if I could make the right turn necessary to get back on the highway. "No, I will need to back up and get away from this divider first."

He graciously offered, "Give me some time, and I will get traffic backed up so you have room to come back far enough to make the turn to the right. Then go about two blocks and you will see the sign for route 22. If you turn left, it will take you out of town."

"Thank you so much! I had no idea what to do, and I am so thankful for your help." A challenge can come because of a confusing situation. Being alert to signs along the way is so important, especially in a town where signs are everywhere that have nothing to do with what highway or street you're on.

Getting ready to leave Allentown, Pennsylvania, I was planning my route to a shipper in Philadelphia and noted the customer directions ended with "Pier 78." I tried not to be intimidated, but I pictured cranes lifting cargo off of ships as I had seen in the movies, where the pier was always a dangerous place to be. But when I found my way to the guard shack, I saw a sign, "Pier 78," on the corner of the most beautiful, white, clean warehouse I had ever seen. As I was driving up to the building, I saw a ship docked right next to it. As I walked past the ship to the office, it was totally outside of my realm of experience. At the same time, it was fascinating for me to look up at the huge ship, which was also white. Other than the ship, it was the same as docking at any warehouse. I got one picture from just past the guard shack, but when I got out to take a picture of my truck backed up to it, I was stopped by the guard.

He said simply, "No pictures."

"Is that because of 9/11?" I asked.

"I'm not sure, but that's probably the reason. I just know I'm not supposed to allow it."

Waiting in the office, truckers from the east explained that the warehouse floors matched the decks of the ship, so the fork lifts went right from the warehouse into the ship and unloaded it similarly to how they would unload a semi-trailer. Because they lived near the coast, this setup was not unusual for them, but for me, living in the Midwest all my life, it was a new, fascinating experience. I felt the same way in South Carolina talking with local truckers about how they got the huge bales of cotton onto a truck. They couldn't believe I didn't know anything about cotton until I told them I was from Iowa. "Why do the bales of cotton sit out in the fields?" I asked. One driver said he had the cotton catch fire on his truck because it wasn't dry enough. When I was young, if a farmer was not patient enough to wait for the hay to be completely dry, he might lose his barn due to spontaneous combustion. Maybe it's one reason you can see so much hay stored in large bales outside in the western states.

It was very dark early in the morning on my way to a receiver in the northern Chicago suburb of Gurnee, when the thought crossed my mind to find a place to park when I got close to the suburb. Maybe I should wait for daylight, as I hadn't been to the warehouse. I now know it was a wise thought that I chose to ignore. When I got to the warehouse, I turned wide as usual to get in the driveway and suddenly felt the ground dip. When I tried to turn out of it, I felt my truck start to lean too far to the left. I thought the truck was going to tip over and stopped. When I got out the passenger side I saw two wheels of the trailer were up in the air off the driveway! It took two wreckers to pull me out while stabilizing the trailer. The drive didn't match the entrance, but turned back to the right. There was no way for me to see that in the dark. If I had listened to wisdom, I would have saved my company a lot of money and saved me much anxiety.

An important part of trucking is the equipment. Having an alternator go out was not fun. The company I worked for at the time liked to make their own repairs to save money, so I needed to get back to the company, even if the truck only allowed me to drive slowly. It didn't allow me to downshift, which was a major problem on the hills. It finally quit on the last hill before my exit, and I barely got the truck to the shoulder. A mechanic came out, made a temporary fix, and followed me to the shop to make sure I got there safely. At some point one just can't expect that much out of a seven-year old truck with almost a million miles on the odometer. When I was assigned a truck at my current company, I got a 2007 Volvo. One of the important reasons I enjoy this company is their policy of selling any truck with close to five hundred thousand miles on it. They also sell the trailers after three or four years. The equipment I have to work with seldom breaks down, and all the moving parts lack the rust of some of the vehicles at former companies, making my job easier.

At times truckers encounter other drivers doing things we can't anticipate, but which are dangerous. Along the way back to Iowa, a careless, risky, illegal maneuver happened near Salina, Kansas. As I was headed east and about to exit I-70, a car was coming toward me on my side of the interstate going the wrong way. I laid on my horn as she went past me, and then she did a U-turn and followed me up the exit ramp. At the top of the ramp, I was going right and she was going left. I looked over and saw a woman with her hand over her mouth. I might have scared her and maybe that was okay. I don't know how she got there, but she may have tried to beat me to the exit ramp, because she was headed right at me. It takes the length of a football field to stop a semi with a loaded trailer at highway speeds. Although I had slowed down for the exit, we were both fortunate that she got safely off the interstate without a horrendous accident.

One spring night I came out of Ottumwa, Iowa, and had to meet a driver who had my truck. We were going to switch trucks so I could get back in my own truck after a repair. She was parked up near Clear Lake, Iowa. A storm was coming, but I didn't meet the rain until shortly after leaving Ottumwa. I got safely to Altoona, Iowa, to fuel my tractor. When I was finished and went in to sign for the fuel, the sky opened up, soaking me in the fifteen feet to the door. I didn't have a dry pocket to put the receipt in. The storm was not quite done with me. After changing clothes, I drove through standing water to get out to the interstate. It was completely black out, and the rain was blowing sideways so there were little waves of water crossing the road. The radio warned of flash flooding and later of severe thunderstorms. I thought I was past the heaviest rain and looked forward to the weather clearing up. Before I got to Ames, Iowa, I moved into the left lane because cars had their flashers on in the right lane. As I got closer, I saw a car in the median. I wondered if the driver had panicked in the downpour, but as I looked back at my lane, I couldn't see the dotted line. Uh-oh. Even though I was going only fifty miles per hour, I hit the water and created an upside-down waterfall that obliterated my visibility for several seconds. I didn't want to stay in the water and I knew I was on a straight stretch of road, so I just kept on going. It was pretty scary. Later I found several occasions to brake to make sure my brakes were dried out. There is no way to change the weather, but in severe weather it pays to be alert to any indication of a change. It was good I had already slowed.

For one of my reloads, I was to pick up the trailer at the shipper immediately and bring it to another trucker who would deliver it. I told dispatch I had to stop and fuel. "You don't have time! You need to get to the shipper now. The other truck is waiting for it." While I'm not always an assertive person, I objected. But when I was met with resistance, I skipped the fuel stop. At the shipper, it took fifteen minutes to find the trailer. They said it was still in the dock. Fifteen minutes is all the time it takes fuel my truck. I took the trailer to the other trucker—well, not quite. Eleven miles short of him, I ran out of fuel while turning from one highway to another. Luckily, no vehicles were coming my way. When the engine stops, so does the power steering. I knew I couldn't get the wheel turned enough to get to the right shoulder. The second-best option was the shoulder on the opposite side of the road. I had just enough muscle to get it over there while coasting, getting off the roadway, and parking the trailer and cab in a straight line. Then I called dispatch to relay the news, so someone there could make a new plan. A person from dispatch contacted the other driver to bring me enough fuel to go eleven miles. One moment of doubt about how well I did under the circumstances was when a patrol car came by, but he didn't even stop to ask why I was on the wrong side of the road. It turned out there were two drivers who bought containers and filled them with fuel for me. They were gracious about the delay and had already speculated correctly on what had happened. The older one said, "The next time someone tells you not to fuel up, tell them okay, then stop and fuel up your truck. You are the only one who knows what your truck needs." I've always thought of running out of fuel as a matter of embarrassment. That afternoon I found out it is actually a matter of my safety, and I will not comply with another request without considering what is best for my truck.

One hot summer evening I encountered a problem when I parked my truck. All the trailer lights went out. It didn't make sense, and while I was trying to solve that problem, I noticed the right window wouldn't go down. Then all the information on the dash disappeared: speedometer, odometer, fuel level, air pressure, tachometer, temperature levels of oil, water, etc. Lastly, the air conditioning stopped. A call to the shop confirmed it was a serious problem, and I would have to drive the twenty-nine miles to the shop as soon as it was daylight. It was scary, but I made it on three little-used roads early enough when traffic was light. It turned out a grounding wire was loose. Without a good ground, all kinds of problems appeared—kind of like we are when we don't stay grounded in Jesus Christ and the Word of God and find ourselves struggling.

One night I was driving north on I-35 toward Des Moines, Iowa. I was about forty miles from the receiver and had just enough hours to get there. A very long hill goes down into Des Moines. On the way down, I noticed the engine light come on. Then I couldn't seem to downshift at all. My load was heavy enough to brake on the way down, but before I could pull over I had to get past cars merging from the right. I stopped braking to save enough momentum. As I started to pull over, I realized my power steering was gone. "What is wrong with my truck?" I said in confusion. When I came to a stop, I could tell the truck wasn't running. It looked as though I might spend the night on the side of the interstate, but when I turned the key, the truck started right up. I gingerly pulled ahead a bit, then put on my left signal and headed toward the receiver in Boone, Iowa. I got all the way there without any further problem. I still didn't know what had gone on.

I slept at the receiver and delivered the load without incident. It was still a mystery. I went from there to western Iowa to pick up another load. On the way across Iowa, my cruise control kept shutting off. I had complained two days before and was told to try lifting up on the clutch pedal. That had worked, so I was able to have the air conditioner on to sleep. I used that technique across Iowa, but in the quiet, I began to piece together the advice with what went wrong on that hill in Des Moines. I problem-solved what would happen if the clutch pedal had dropped. In a car, you can push in the clutch and the car will run continuously. If you stop a truck for a length of time, you need to set the brake and bump the idle speed up to keep it running. When I went down the hill the night before, the clutch pedal dropped and my truck reacted as if it were in neutral, so the motor then quit. My reefer was running so I didn't notice that my truck was off. The warning light, not downshifting, no power steering—all are things consistent with the engine being off. Luckily, flashers work anytime. The only reason I figured it out going across Iowa was because my reefer wasn't running when the trailer was empty. Every time the cruise shut off, I heard the change in the motor, put my foot under the clutch, and pulled it up. I did that so many times that I advised my dispatcher of the problem. She thought it was something that needed to get fixed and called the shop to let them know I had to come in. The mechanic listened to the symptoms I described and got to work. Fifteen minutes later he was done and showed me the problem. It was a single loop spring, which had become weak from use and no longer kept the clutch up when my foot was taken off of it. It was about the size of my hand and wreaked havoc that night in Des Moines. Thank goodness for the wisdom of the mechanics and the wisdom of the Spirit given me on my way across Iowa.

In April 2009, I had unexpectedly made it to my cousin's son's confirmation and saw his Bible verse was 1 Corinthians 10:13. When I read the verse in the bulletin, it ended with "a way of escape." When he said it aloud during the service, he said it as "a way out," from another version of the Bible. The phrase immediately sounded like a title of a poem I should write. "A Way Out" was a perfect title for a poem about a close call driving on I-94 in Michigan, yet it took another two and a half years before it was written.

Every trucker faces challenges continually. When the instructors at the training school told us they learned something new every day, I found it hard to believe because they had many years of experience and were so knowledgeable. Now I understand what they were talking about, and I know next week will bring new challenges for me. If you ask teachers, they also face challenges all the time, whether it is unmotivated students, parents who need to be contacted for some reason, new research that they are asked to implement, their workload with its deadlines, or relationships with their superiors. In any career, and with whatever challenges life presents, keeping a close relationship with God will help get through the hard times.

Lord, You and I both know I could never do this job without You and the thoughts given me to handle an unexpected challenge or impending hazard. When I think of a solution for something I know nothing about, I know it's Your idea. I know You love me and want to keep me from harm. I don't have words enough to express my gratitude for the way You take care of me out here alone. In need of You, amen.

Stress Less

At times it's hard to believe what I do
At 5'4" the truck is twice my height
When I wrestle with a door latch
That doesn't move just right
Tug on the lever to move trailer wheels
Pull on the release of the fifth wheel lock
Or wind the handle to move legs up/down
I'm amazed that I am doing this work

It's not just the needed strength to work
Sometimes I need to work long hours
That's not a change for me from teaching
Sleep is extremely important in trucking
Eating at regular times is not possible
Keeping hydrated at all times is necessary
Staying alert to the highway world is crucial
No one else can cover for you in this job

I work in a world dominated by men
Some less intelligent, but more experienced
In this world I find I need to present an image
Of a professional to prevent the inappropriate
It helps develop a mutual respect with drivers
I have found that if they see I am trying
To solve my own problem first, before asking
They are always willing to help me out

Though I have almost always enjoyed solitude
At times it is lonely work far from home
Decisions often made with input from no one
There are unwritten company/dispatch rules

Semi Serious

I have learned and still need to learn
The unknown is the most frustrating part
When there's no one to give advice
I may still have to endure a reprimand

The world of trucking is an objective one
There is very little subjectivity in this work
You are on time or you are late
You are a legal weight or overweight
You drive the speed limit or you are speeding
The directions are correct or you get lost
Your logs are up to date or you are illegal
Your license is current or you park your truck

It is far different than the world of teaching
When I was teaching, it was always with me
Nights and weekends gave me no break
The world of trucking means I am done
Whenever the wheels are stopped
Yes, I have to update the log–ten minutes
There are stresses, but they are momentary
This makes it less stressful than teaching

2009

A Way Out

The school calls it managing your space
"Make sure you give yourself a way out."
Stopping a semi takes three hundred feet
More for a heavy load or bad weather

I leave a football field in front of me
It's a safety cushion for reaction time
Four Chicago drivers fit into my space
The fifth car gladly slips in behind me

None of us has to brake for the merge
I keep my slower speed and gradually
My cushion is soon back to its size
Not sure why it always works in Chicago

One day on an interstate in Michigan
Driving to a shipper with an empty trailer
I was in the left lane in heavy traffic
My three hundred feet were in place

I caught a glimpse of flashing lights
A patrol car ahead on the right shoulder
Three semis on my right, so I braked
If they wanted to move into my lane

The first one signaled and came over
The other two were following too close
Seeing the lights late, they moved over
No signal and my space became twenty

Semi Serious

I was still slowing to regain my cushion
When the truck ahead of me braked
Focusing on patrol car and trailer ahead
I began to move toward the right lane

Time moved so slowly but at warp speed
As the trucker in front moved to the left
Raising dust as he braked on the shoulder
No time to check what was behind me

I slipped past patrol car and his customer
Missed the edge of the trailer in front
By a couple of feet and caught a glimpse
Of the truck behind taking to the shoulder

Two cars and *five* semi trucks safe
But probably as shook up as I was
Dust in the air and the smell of brakes
But with the cushion, none of us touched

Thankful for the outstanding advice
I told the story to the training director
I knew the dry roads and empty trailer
Also helped avoid an injury disaster

A short time after that close call
I was at a relative's confirmation
His Bible verse was about temptation
And God providing a way of escape

When he recited the verse up front
He used the words *a way out*
As soon as he spoke the words I knew
It was a title of a poem yet written

But the verse has further application
I leave myself a way out on the highway
But the rest of the time off the road
I need to look out for what tempts me

2011

"Keep on trucking"
Whatever the weather, rain, snow, fog, flooded lots, truckers just keep working.

"Flooded Dock after Downpour"
After a nap, I woke up to changed circumstances!

"Where is the Street?"
Moving to a truck stop to dry out my boots was a new experience.

"Unique Load"
"This one auger took two forklifts and three people problem solving to get it out of the trailer."

Top Ten Things Trucking Taught Me about Trucking and about Life

10. Start every day with an inspection of my vehicle. (I start each day with prayer, some Scripture reading, and moments of silent listening.)

9. Plan my route; how many miles, where to stop for a break, and directions to my destination. (What are some things I want to accomplish today, how long will it take, will it move me toward my ultimate destination, and does God have a plan for me?)

8. Stay centered in my lane. (When I stay centered in Christ, I will learn from His wisdom.)

7. Scan the ditches. In deer season, especially at dawn and dusk, I watch for any animal. (When I watch for temptations, I can avoid them.)

6. Read the signs. Weigh station signs were hard for me at first. Driving by an open weigh station is not good. (In life there are so-called red flags, signs to help me know the choice to make. Some people in the Bible asked for signs, and some people ignored signs.)

5. I can only drive my own truck. (It's hard enough to live my own life. I don't need to try to change how someone else is living theirs.)

4. When facing a storm, slow down and evaluate. Can I see a lighter sky to move toward or do I stop until the worst is over? (We all face storms in life. Sometimes we can move through it, and sometimes we need to seek the shelter of God's love until the worst is over.)

3. Never out-drive my headlights. Whether it is darkness, fog, a downpour, or a snowstorm, I need to slow down so I can see a hazard in time to stop. (Life is most troublesome when I can't see my way out of a situation. I must go carefully to avoid making a bad situation worse.)

2. The trucking school called it managing your space. Be aware of the vehicles around me, if it gets crowded on the highway, hang back a bit. Don't follow too closely. (Jesus is the one to follow. His ways are always the right way. Follow Him closely.)

1. I can't do it without help and support from my company. (Prayer partners are invaluable. God, His Son, Jesus, and His Holy Spirit are with me all the time and will help if I seek them and sometimes when I don't.)

"A Light at the End of the Tunnel"
"It was an extremely slow day for traffic in
Pennsylvania when I took this picture.
I have never been in a tunnel alone before or after this shot."

7

Encouragement

> Therefore encourage one another and build one
> another up, just as you are doing.
> —1 Thessalonians 5:11

Five or six days a week I get to enjoy the various sunrises and sunsets in the most panoramic proportions. The night in the winter months is long, but in those months I can often see both the sunrise and sunset in the same day. They are more brilliant if clouds are in the sky. The clouds extend the area of color and often provide different hues and shades. One fall day, I was driving on highway 151 in Wisconsin heading east and watching a gorgeous sunrise that rivaled many sunsets I've seen. Plenty of clouds accented the colors, and I could see the sunrise in my mirror reaching all 360 degrees of the horizon. I kept my sunglasses and cap ready as I got closer to Madison's morning rush hour. After a brief appearance, the sun ducked back behind some other clouds and continued its amazing display of colors. After seventy-five minutes, the colors turned to blues and grays; they were still beautiful, but technically not part of the sunrise. Sometimes this job has rewards that have no price. It's hard to miss a sunrise or sunset amidst the clouds. It occurred to me it's the same with God. When there are some clouds in my life, God is more visible to me. It's hard to miss Him as I weave my way through the problems and feel His counsel and support.

In Pennsylvania on I-76, there is a stretch in the mountains that has three tunnels within 13.1 miles. Once when I was still a rookie, the air was heavy on me in the third and last tunnel. The lights were making me nauseous and my breath came almost in gasps, so as soon as I got through it, I pulled over until my breathing became normal. Now as I go through them I note how long each tunnel is and how many miles from first to last and I notice things about the vehicles sharing the tunnel with me. The walls of the tunnel concern me no more than the white line at the edge of any highway. This is one job where I can see objectively how much better I am than when I started.

Traveling near Fond du Lac, Wisconsin, on a windy afternoon, a garbage can lid came rolling down a driveway on a collision course with my trailer wheels. Traffic wouldn't allow me to avoid it, and I felt badly that I would surely destroy it. Looking in my right side mirror, I saw one of my wheels neatly clip it and flip it so it landed unscathed at the bottom of the driveway. I confess I pumped my fist as if I had planned it that way.

One warm summer day at the end of a long week, I had to take a ten-hour break, and I couldn't start for home because I had used up the seventy hours for the week. The next day I would pick up some more hours. I parked at a truck stop a few blocks away, and I thought of going in for a hot breakfast and doing devotions at a real table, but I was so tired I slept. After doing my log, texting my daughter and a friend, I added up the miles and realized why I was so tired. By the time I parked my rig, I'd put on 2,670 miles in the six days, and all of them were through the night. I slept again without setting an alarm for the first time all week. It meant getting home later than I wanted to, but the ride home was easier because I was well rested. Yes, it was a tough week, but you know what? The solution to my exhaustion was simple—sleep. The thing I like about trucking is it's an objective job. This week I was early to every trip, but it didn't matter if I was eight hours ahead of my appointment like at St. Michael, Minnesota, or if I was five minutes ahead of my appointment at Council Bluffs, Iowa. It only mattered that I was on time. I don't have to wonder if I did my job right. Even the five-minute leeway was no cause for regret. I was on time—period. Yes, I worried before I got there, but once I was checked in at 5:55 a.m., it was no longer a concern for me. I had done my job right.

I have to mention a great compliment I got one week when I delivered a load near our company to a farm with a tight dock area. After he'd unloaded my trailer, the farmer mentioned I was only the second driver who backed into the dock on the first try. The other driver was our shag driver who delivered there all the time. What a great encouragement!

My son-in-law and I traded vehicles one week so he could take my car to Texas to see his family and save on gas. When I got to the driver's lot at my company, it took me awhile to find my "car." Later as I was finishing up my fast-food supper in the motel parking lot where drivers are allowed to sleep, a young woman approached me and wondered if I could jump-start her car. She had the cables. Silently, I wished I had memorized those steps: which came first, red or black, and which vehicle was first.

"Let me finish these two bites and I'll be right over. This is my son-in-law's pickup and I'll call him to make sure we do all the steps right." My first question to him was "How do you open your hood?" I found the latch that popped it, but couldn't get it to open. The young woman got it open for me. He led me through the process, and I hung up. She and I talked while we waited for the battery to charge. It turned out she had worked temporarily at my company in the office. When her car started, we looked at the instructions on the cables as to how to undo the connection and found out my memory was correct. She and I had a giggling good time, and when we successfully got her cables undone, we said in unison, "We did it!" I texted a thank-you to my son-in-law and told him he made me look good.

It feels so good to help someone out, even if it is just the smallest thing. As I pulled out of a dock in Chicago, I turned the opposite way from when I came in. When I was closing my doors, a driver whose truck was still in a dock came over and asked why I was going the other way. I told him the warehouse man had given me directions to get out of Chicago without going through the construction on I-290. The driver thanked me, and I was sure he would find it an easy way out of the area.

Working through a holiday is not unusual for a trucker. After sitting in a truck stop all day, driving into Chicago the evening of July 4, 2010, was an amazing experience. First, I was thinking Sunday night—piece of cake. Oops! It could have been worse. Though there was quite a bit of traffic, it moved at the speed limit. Fireworks were already starting all over. Some of them were bursting right near the interstate, which was a thrill. Close to downtown, there were three or four places where people were setting them off, and as I got to my exit, the brake lights and the sounds of the fireworks added up to a lot of adrenaline. Don't know that I want to repeat that trip, but it was a memory maker. The next day I got to spend twenty-four hours in a truck stop all day again because my reload warehouse wasn't open. At least the air conditioning in that truck stop was working compared with the day before in a different town. My laundry got done, and in the process I had a nice long two-hour conversation with two other women truckers (also doing their laundry). We covered a wide range of subjects: trucking, families, other jobs we'd had, a smidgen of politics, religion, education today, men, hard times, and heartaches. We didn't leave anything out. We will probably never see each other again, but that's okay. After two twenty-four-hour periods of sitting, I really needed something to perk me up. Those two women were a real blessing, which was something my pastor and her husband had prayed for. They also are a blessing for me.

After dropping my empty trailer down the street from a warehouse in Ottumwa, I came back to the entrance, which was in the process of reconstruction. It was unclear which lane I should be in. A woman came out and signaled to me, and I moved to the correct lane. Then I parked my bobtail, and she came out again and asked me to park past the gate. As I walked into the guardhouse, I joked with the security guard, "I seem to need a lot of help tonight." While I waited for the woman to ask for my information, he mentioned they had been busy. "She was patient with me, so I will be patient with her." I spoke to the guard, but I noticed a smile come to her face as she finished her task at hand. Later, as I was trying to hook up to my trailer, it was too low for me to fit under. I had tried to wind up the legs in low gear, but couldn't budge the forty-thousand-pound trailer. I called the guardhouse number, asked for help, and waited. A shag driver was there almost immediately—an unheard of speed in a warehouse lot. I will never know for sure, but I suspect the woman appreciated my patience and returned the favor. People in the transportation industry are just like everyone else. Treat others with respect, and they will in turn respect you.

In Bolingbrook, Illinois, I arrived in the wee hours shortly after midnight, but didn't get loaded until 6 a.m. The load was due in Minneapolis at 1 p.m. I took off right away, gave up my bonus for holding my speed down and arrived at 1:15. The man in the warehouse looked defeated when he saw me waiting with my paperwork. He warned me it would be a long time. Being out of hours anyway, it didn't matter to me. I asked what truck was ahead of me, but he didn't know, just that there were five ahead of me. Back outside, I walked along the line of trucks writing down the company name of each truck. One of the drivers had his window open, so I told him what I was doing. He let me know which two trucks were here when he came and he knew the order of the next two who came after him. By the time I was done sorting out who was next in the dock and in what order, several of us were outside our trucks chatting. Two more trucks had pulled in before I finished. One of the new drivers came out after talking to the warehouse man and told us we were all supposed to come in at 2 p.m. If we didn't come in, we might lose our place, because the warehouse man had to write down the order of unloading for the next shift. I asked which truck he was and told him he was seventh, and then I told the other drivers I was going to put the list on paper (instead of on the palm of my hand). When the man came out at 2 p.m., the drivers pointed to me and said, "The teacher has the list. She's got us all organized." I think he was expecting some bickering, but realized we all agreed on the order. He went back inside with my list. We stayed outside our trucks chatting until we got cold. It was awesome to be respected.

At a place for dropping the loaded trailer and picking up an empty, the last line of the dispatch said there was a self-serve washout right there. I figured I would try it, so I wouldn't have to take extra time to find a washout place. The first thing I noticed was the on/off switch was about ten feet from the trailer, so I took the two-inch-diameter hose and hoisted as much of it as I could up into the trailer. It wasn't easy because it wanted to slide right back out, but I finally got what I thought I needed to stay in the trailer. Then I moved a set of steps over. Because both doors were open, it was the only way for me to get up into the trailer without the handle on the left door. The sign by the switch said keep a good grip on the hose because the water was under high pressure. My grip was fine—my aim not so much. Luckily, no one was around to hit.

Getting up the steps while controlling the hose went quite well. I got to the nose of the trailer (way up front) and found I was about six feet short of hose. I tried to use it from a distance, but realized it wasn't going to get the front clean. I turned to look at the hose behind me and saw the hose was exactly the same width as the grooves in the floor of my trailer and it was stuck down in one. As I turned around to fix the problem, the high-pressure water hit the side closest to me and gave me my first shower. It took a lot of coaxing to get the hose out of the groove it was in, and I occasionally lost track of the aim of the end of the hose, showering myself intermittently. I got to the back of the trailer and managed to pull up some additional hose so I wouldn't have to repeat this task again. I was careful to keep the hose out of the grooves by winding it side to side, but by this time I was feeling pretty much as though I were in an *I Love Lucy* episode. Going back up to the front of the trailer, I discovered that because the water coming out of the hose was hot and I had taken so much time getting the hose to behave, the front of the trailer was so hot and humid, the steam rendered my glasses useless. I stuck them down on the end of my nose and washed the trailer semi blind. Every time I thought I was getting the hang of it, I'd get wet again. I was getting tired of wrestling this hose that seemed to have a life of its own. Finally, I was making my way to the rear of the trailer and was able to see again. Then out of the corner of my eye I noticed another semi parked behind me. I hoped the driver hadn't seen the worst of the Lucy antics.

As I finished the end of the trailer, I tried to hose out the holes that allow the water to drain out of the trailer. Well, that had the same effect as hitting the side of the trailer, only with dirty water spewing up and all over me. I thought I was done and noticed the other driver signaling me. So I washed the end of the trailer back and forth in the directions he indicated, but it seemed to be clean. Finally, he leaned out the window and over the sound of the hose, yelled for me to clean his windshield. I was glad he didn't make any comment about my obvious lack of skill. The least he could have done is shut off the water, but he was probably wise not to get anywhere near my range of motion. I was thankful I had at least thought ahead enough to put on my boots, a shirt I didn't care about, and a pair of my oldest jeans. Nonetheless, I informed dispatch I was in bad need of a shower after ridding the trailer of raw meat pieces and blood. My daughter wished a video camera had been around, because YouTube would have loved it. Maybe after I was clean and dry, it might have been fun to watch, but not at that moment.

Friday, January 22, 2010, I waited for a reload at Grand Island, Nebraska. The call I got mentioned a load to Oregon that needed to be covered. Although no snow was on the ground in Nebraska, I told the dispatcher I had never been to Oregon in the semi and had no desire to go. Her boss called me later and asked me to drive fifty miles east and wake up the driver with the load for Oregon. He said they were trying to get a relay arranged to take it from me partway. He mentioned I might have to go all the way to Oregon. "I don't think that's a good idea," I said calmly. He asked me if I had chains. "No." Then he told me to tell the other driver to put his chains on my truck. "I don't even know how to put chains on," I told him. He was sure another driver would help and maybe I could pay him twenty-five dollars to put my chains on. I pictured myself at the top of a mountain pass with ten other truckers on the side of the road trying to put their chains on. Guys don't mind helping a woman trucker if they see she has tried to solve the problem on her own. This is not a career for the helpless type of woman because the men sometimes feel taken advantage of. My boss finally asked me to give my phone to the other driver, and I was happy to do that.

I was calm through the entire discussion of the dilemma of this load. I was aware of a lack of fear, which struck me as odd, even as I imagined driving over the Rockies, in a big rig, in January, with a snowstorm predicted to hit at least part of the route. It was a situation I'd always said would never happen, even in summer. Though I felt no fear, I prayed, "I don't think this is a good idea, and if You agree with me, I need You to intervene." Then I ate a sandwich and lay down in the bunk to wait for a decision to be made. Soon I heard another truck pull up and heard voices. It was a third driver from my company. He'd come from thirty miles away, and they rearranged their bunks and personal items to put both of them in one truck to team drive that load to Oregon.

I was thankful it was done without me. There was no huge feeling of relief in me, just a "That makes more sense" thought. I was left with "Where was my fear?" It was totally out of character for me. I should have been filled with anxiety and close to tears. Then I realized I had not felt fear for some time. In that time, I'd driven on snow-covered roads, in drifting snow, and in dense fog, sometimes seeing only seventy-five feet in front of me both in Kansas and most of Minnesota and Wisconsin, where the fog built up two inches of white ice on my mirrors. I even took a picture with my ruler to prove it. Then I had driven in freezing drizzle from Wisconsin to just past Iowa City (one-third of the way toward Nebraska). That impressed the broker the next morning when I let him know I'd make my appointment on time. A trucker who parked beside me that morning had four inches of pure ice on his mirrors. He assured me the roads were better going west than the day before when he got the ice on his mirrors. In all that time, I didn't notice the lack of fear.

I had to look back to a prayer my pastor prayed with the whole congregation responding. It was a prayer I had heard but not prayed earnestly. By that time, I had developed a trust in my pastor, so when she ended the prayer with "Jesus, I ask You to come into my heart," I said it with conviction. That prayer had a profound effect on me two weeks later during that phone call in Nebraska, as evidenced by the peace I felt that day. I have no doubt I can lose that peace at any time, and I have a few times since then. The difference is that once I had felt that peace, it was hard to be without it. The way back is to get centered in Christ again. I didn't realize until months later when I was typing up a poem the Lord helped me write and saw the date by my signature, January 11, 2010, which meant it was written the very next morning after I said that prayer. "Praise for the Heavens" was the poem I wanted to write, but I couldn't even get a start on it. Finally, I just told God, "Lord, You know what I want to include in this poem, but I can't seem to get it started, so I give it to You." I went to bed. At 3 a.m. I woke up and had the first verse, so I got out a pad of paper and wrote. The rest of it just flowed out of the pen.

One spring, my pastor wondered if I'd like to sing in the cantata our choir was doing on Palm Sunday. While I was processing the whole "When would I get to practice?" thought, she showed me a CD with the whole cantata on it and thought I could listen in the truck and learn it. It was a bright spot in each day as I left the fog behind in Iowa and traded it for the dreary rain that followed me to Virginia and back. Rain, however, does not slow me down the way fog does and doesn't leave me exhausted—just irritated as everything about the outside of the truck is wet and some wetness finds its way inside the truck. But learning that cantata seemed to make the fog, rain, and wetness irrelevant. As I sang along, I experimented with my voice, trying to imitate the fullness of those singers. I also practiced breath control until I could hold a note as long as those on the CD did. It changed my voice, and even now once in a while I don't recognize my voice when I sing because it has fullness and a strength it hasn't had before. The next year, during Lent, I played that CD and discovered I remembered most of it and was able to sing along with it. Every so often I get a text from my pastor that says, "Keep singing." It is an uplifting reminder of those days.

Dear Lord, thank You for all the ways You have encouraged me as I travel this nation's roadways. I ask You to give me a nudge to reach out to others so I might make a difference in whatever way I am able, while still fulfilling my responsibilities. I am grateful for those who have shown me patience and understanding. Help me treat others in a way that brings honor to You. With a joyful song, amen.

The Song of the Trailer

When the wind is just right
Not too strong
But more than a breeze
The trailer sings to me
As I open the doors or
When fueling my tractor
Or just walking by

I sometimes stop and listen
To the various notes
It plays with the wind
Season or month matter not
The songs come in January chill
March's new spring warmth
Or heat of coming June storm

Today I fueled at a small
Quiet truck stop at home
The engine turned off
Fuel was slowly flowing
And I listened to notes
Moving randomly up and down
In a kind of lonely song

I've never heard anyone
Talk about the trailer's song
Truckers are mostly men
Who are just itching
To get the wheels moving
Perhaps they don't notice
Or think it's anything special

The poet in me was moved
As I listened and wondered
How it is that the trailer
Can perform this mystery
Not every trailer does
Perhaps the older it is
The better the song

2009

Praise for the Heavens

O Lord, the heavens reflect Your glory
From childhood I have seen the sky
Full of endless stars in the night
Or moonlight that dims the starlight
I stood in awe of the immense space
Aware of how small my father and I were

Dad taught me to watch for storms
Which clouds brought torrents of rain
Which clouds might bring danger
Of high winds or even tornadoes
Years later I led canoes to safety
Before an approaching cloudburst

Lord, You surprise and delight me
With the endless variety of colors
Splashed outside my windshield
Whether sunrise with its subtle hues
The bright, gaudy colors of a sunset
Or calm colors of the moon amidst clouds

I've seen thunderheads build up high
And felt the pounding wind and rain
As it bore down and rocked my truck
The lessons learned from my father
Remain true as I study the clouds
For the dangerous colors to avoid

Lord, You send the clouds to bring rain
Clouds that empty themselves for naught
Over a dry and parched western state

As the moisture evaporates into the air
But I know there will be another day
When you send the rain the ground needs

In winter I see You paint the trees
With a crystalline, shimmering coat of ice
Trees barren of leaves grow beautiful
As the frigid air changes the rain
Or powders the branches, bare or green
With the white frost from the morning fog

Lord, You bring water to the earth
Stored as snow for a time in winter
Your provision of moisture for the future
Needs to be respected by people on earth
For that which brings the green of spring
Can hurt or kill those too casual with it

Even in winter You bring the colors
When a rainbow suddenly appears
As I travel through a light bank of fog
Mini rainbows may appear beside the sun
On an extremely cold day; while at night
The moon is circled with a ring of color

Lord, You can do anything You want
Like the heavy clouded sky at dusk
That showed no promise for a sunset
But You changed it into a brilliance
As You parted the clouds just enough
To present me with an evening show

Lord, You gave us the sun to warm us
The sun we crave on short winter days
The sun we seek to escape in summer.
You gave us the moon to glow at night
The moon I long to see when driving
 Through a long night on the road

> 2010

"Early Sunrise"
"Caught this picture one foggy morning from
a small truck stop near Early, IA"

"Trucker Sunset"
"I love all sunsets, but most are recorded
in my head. This one is special."

8
The Seasons

> For everything there is a season and a time
> for every matter under heaven.
> —Ecclesiastes 3:1

Each season has its beauty and its ugliness. Spring brings new life to flora and fauna. Buds and blossoms appear on the trees, the grass greens the roadsides and meadows, and baby animals appear on farms. Wildlife mothers tend to keep their offspring out of sight, but I have seen many fawns and even a baby buffalo. More often I see baby ducks, geese, pheasants, and even young turkeys. Tornadoes and hurricanes can tear into spring and leave a whole landscape ruined. Floods often come as a result of those storms, destroying crops and stranding wildlife.

In summer, the earth's vegetation matures, and the baby animals grow up. In drier parts of the country, grass fires or forest fires leave the earth black and scorched. One dry summer, driving north in Oklahoma, I literally saw rain evaporate before it got to the ground. It was pouring out of two clouds, but the streaks ended well short of relieving the drought.

With fall comes the beauty of the leaves. As I drive around the country, I sometimes get to see the colors several times, depending on temperature, location, and elevation. There is not much ugly about autumn, except after the colors, comes the fade of fall when the grass turns brown and the tree branches become bare.

Winter frost, snow, and ice are gorgeous on the trees and bushes, turning the whole world into a Christmas card. When the burden of ice or snow is too heavy, the branches begin to break, leaving ugly scars and trees misshaped.

Through the beauty of the seasons, I thank and praise God for His creation. Through the ugliness of the seasons, I pray for those affected. Most are in places where I know no one, but God knows exactly who needs the prayers, and I leave the details to Him.

Many times when I am driving my big rig, I find myself wishing family and friends were riding with me to share the experience. Last spring I was in Pennsylvania, Maryland, and northern Virginia one week. The following week it was southern Illinois, Kentucky, Tennessee, and southern Virginia. Blossoms were in many colors, such as the violet redbud and white dogwood, but also rust, yellow, and orange blossoms on unidentified trees. It was almost as if they were giving me a preview of the colors to come in the fall. The mountain hillsides were full of every conceivable shade of green you could imagine. All of it was covering the hills and mountains with new life. These scenes in the mountains gave me picture after picture of landscape paintings or photographs that I cannot adequately capture. I've tried, but I will have to settle for enjoying them in the moment and hope my mental pictures stay strong. One of the reasons the mountains fascinate me so much is my home state of Iowa doesn't have many places where I can see rock formations, either natural or man-made. When my routes take me through the mountains, I can see the scars made by engineers many years ago who chiseled out passages for the railroads and later, the interstate system. I marvel at their genius: building roads around the mountains, over rivers, and deep ravines and tunneling as much as a mile through the immense land masses.

It's not just the land formations that vary greatly as I drive through different regions, it's also what grows out of the land. As a farmer's daughter, I take notice of unfamiliar crops as well as the variety of colors of the earth. Spring highlights these differences as the land gets prepared for planting and the new crops begin to emerge. My father planted corn and soybeans in dirt so black that one of his fields caught on fire because of elements of coal in it. Up in North Dakota, the white soil looks too anemic to support the crops of sunflowers and sugar beets. In Oklahoma, I drove past a road construction area where workers had recently gouged out the earth. It was the most beautiful maroon color and most certainly didn't look like dirt to me. In Nebraska, I saw a crop I couldn't identify. I finally found out it was sorghum. Each area of the country has certain crops that are suited to the environment. It makes me think of how God uses people in different ways. Just as each person has unique gifts and talents, each region has different strengths. It's this variety that keeps life, and our food supply, interesting.

With new life comes a certain amount of instability. Even as spring fosters new beginnings, with baby animals being born and plants of all kinds starting to grow, the transition out of the dead of winter brings ever-changing weather that can be problematic. One of the scariest spring weather dangers is tornadoes, and I've had some close misses. One morning, I left a Texas truck stop at 5:30 a.m. I heard later that two tornadoes hit Texas that morning. Ten days later at night in Ohio, the weather radio said the county I was in was under a tornado warning. The rain was so heavy that it was like driving in dense fog. As it cleared, I saw police and fire trucks by a semi that had been flipped on its side by the wind. I kept driving toward the lighter sky. The following night was déjà vu as I drove through Iowa. The counties and towns the weatherman named were unfamiliar to me, but then he said, "This tornado warning includes I-80 exits 107 to 128." I was at mile marker 116! I kept driving toward the lighter sky in the west. The last cloud of the storm was white and had a little curved tail at the end. It made me think of the radar pictures on TV. Weathermen point to it, calling it a hook echo as a place a tornado might develop. The next morning I heard a tornado ripped through Iowa City, doing a lot of damage. One day, about fifteen to twenty miles north of Omaha, I saw the flashing lights of a half dozen patrol cars. Two semi tow trucks were by a cattle truck. Just beyond that was a semi turned over in the median with the cab messed up. Beyond that I saw another semi on its side in a rest stop. It was the last in a line of trucks parked side by side. It was the only one blown over. Later, I found out that fortunately, there had been no deaths.

I drove through Mississippi after Hurricane Katrina hit the south. I was farther north than New Orleans, so I didn't see the damage there. It was dark when I was driving north through Mississippi. My headlights were highlighting some strange things in the trees on either side of the highway. They looked like primitive fort structures first put up by the settlers in the east. Half the trees were broken off at a height of five to ten feet. Though I was twenty miles from the gulf, the tops of the trees were just not there. When I stopped, I was seventy miles from the gulf and still saw topless trees, though not as many. My young waitress said they had winds of 125 miles per hour. Then she added, with a note of sadness, "I haven't gone down to the coast. I just haven't been able to."

In the summer of 2009, I was driving in northeast Iowa when I noticed a crop I didn't recognize in a field. With a closer look, I saw it was a cornfield. The stalks that remained reminded me of the trees I saw in Mississippi after Katrina. I had just heard an interview on the radio with a farmer talking about a hailstorm that went through his farm. "The beans are gone. I'm standing in my field where the corn only comes up to my knees." He also talked about his barn, where all the windows on the west side were broken by golf-ball-size hail. The hail was piled up on the opposite inside wall, which was forty feet from the broken windows. "That gives you an idea of the velocity the hailstones were traveling at," the farmer explained. As I drove past those fields, I saw the devastation he talked about. When he said the beans were gone, he meant literally. All I could see was some semblance of rows with nothing in them. Unbelievable!

Some of spring's weather problems can carry over into summer. In June one year I saw blackened grass in ditches and along the road, not from fires, but from flood waters that stayed too long. Crossing bridges, I looked down on rivers with no banks, because they were so full. Young saplings were bent sideways, pointing downstream, unable to stand erect. Some adult trees lost their footing and bowed low toward the strength of the river. Others fell back toward the bank, exposing their roots to the rushing water.

Especially bad floods occurred in the Midwest in 2011. In places along the Mississippi, farmland was deliberately flooded to save some towns. From the highway, I could see drowned fields on both sides for miles and miles. I often lift up the farmers in prayer as I pass by such images. The floods along the Missouri River were even more horrific. Large sections of

Semi Serious | 83

I-29 were closed in Iowa and Missouri. Along the places I was allowed on the interstate, it sometimes looked like a lake, even though I knew there were thousands of acres of farmland buried under the water. I can't imagine what those farmers endured to have lost their farms for the entire season. One day in Missouri, I saw numerous pieces of farm machinery. It looked as though farmers were getting ready to sell their equipment. Then later, as I went by some machines alongside a small gravel road with grass growing up around them, I suddenly realized farmers had parked their valuable machines on high ground to save them, not to sell them. The connections between Iowa and Nebraska were reduced to just a few bridges. People who worked across the river had to drive way out of the way just to get to work. Truckers also had to take long detours, and when we were allowed on I-29, we drove between huge bags of gravel on either side of the highway with water lapping just on the other side of them. None of that compared with what the farmers went through.

Driving a semi in the summertime sometimes gives me opportunities to watch the hot thunderstorms of the season in a whole new way. Because my current company hauls meat, I sometimes get to Dodge City, Kansas. The town is a long way from anywhere, despite its fame. I've always loved the West, and I enjoy driving across the empty plains. Montana may be big sky country, but any of those plains states have big skies. I saw a thunderhead cloud that stayed to the west of me for at least sixty miles. It had the classic anvil shape, and somewhere it may have caused some havoc. To the east I spotted a portion of a rainbow that had the most gorgeous violet band on the inside curve. I couldn't ever remember seeing the violet in a rainbow. I called my daughter to ask if violet is the rarest color seen. I wondered if it was the clear, clean air over an area of the plains that has few polluting industries. This country has such a variety of places and people, but the natural creation shouts God-made.

I have come to love the Appalachian Mountains, especially in the fall. While I drove in them for my first company, my second company stayed in the Midwest. Now I again can travel through the mountains. Mountain sides give me the best view of the fall colors. It's like a choir on risers on a stage—everyone can be seen. One time I came around a curve and saw an almost magical set of vivid colors on the mountain. The impact of the scene was strong enough so now every time I drive past that particular spot, I remember the colors. It's moments like this that continue to surprise and delight me and make trucking a most enjoyable career.

Fall is my favorite time of year, but always in the back of my mind is the knowledge that the hardest season for a trucker is just around the corner. My collection of winter driving stories could probably fill its own book, so instead I will just focus on one of the worst encounters I've had with Old Man Winter. In February 2011, we were on the downside of winter—technically speaking! I drove 615 miles January 31 from Haubstadt, Indiana, to ten miles west of Wichita, Kansas. At least four hundred miles were in freezing rain. I ran into it while in St. Louis on I-70. (It almost always rains when I go through St. Louis.) I was looking forward to getting to I-35 and heading south into warmer weather. When I headed south, I had gone only ten miles when it went from thirty degrees to twenty-nine, and the farther south I drove, the colder it got. That's when I realized I was driving deep into the storm that would eventually cover two thousand miles from Texas to New England. I fueled up in Emporia, Kansas. After talking to a trucker coming from Wichita, I headed out on the road again and got to a truck stop a half mile from my delivery destination.

The weather wasn't done with me. The next day, I needed my hammer to get my lock off the trailer because it was frozen. A driver from my company came over to help me open the doors. It was blowing forty to fifty miles per hour, and he didn't want the wind to catch the door and wrench my shoulder. I had to help push the first door open against the wind. The second door was frozen. It's the first time I've seen a problem like that. I've always been amazed at the design of the working parts of a truck that function in all kinds of weather. He got his hammer and banged away at the door. With him pulling on the latch and me pulling on the door, we got it open. The wind was not a factor—the hinges were so frozen, we both had to push to open it all the way, even with the wind helping. I couldn't get the link over the hook to secure the door and then realized there was a half inch of ice on it. One swift hit with the hammer—problem solved.

The warehouse man didn't recommend going back on the road. With our trailers empty, we agreed it would be foolish to try. The other trucker said, "It would be like driving a barn door in the wind." Dispatch said the wind was supposed to die down in the afternoon, so I planned to nap. I could tell from the rocking of my truck, it hadn't died down, so I waited till daylight on February 2. That storm was preceded by winter problems on January 2, 6, 9, 10, 19, and 24 and followed by February 2 and 3 (stuck) and 4 (close to stuck). It was certainly a winter to remember, but it's also one I'd rather forget.

Dear Lord, I love being able to enjoy the seasons You have created for my corner of the world, but I also enjoy seasons in other parts of the country. Thank You for Your protection on those days I have encountered the harshness of winter and the brutal storms of spring. Continue to be with those who have endured destruction from nature. Give them the strength and courage to rebuild their lives after the losses. In Your mercy, amen.

"Storm on the Horizon"
"The anvil shape signals a thunderstorm. I pulled over to take this shot. I see a lot of clouds like this one and sometimes drive into them."

"Dangerous Storm"
"This cloud shook the truck when I drove into it, making me wonder if it preceded a tornado!"

"Rest Stop Wind Damage"
In 2012, a storm with straight line winds caused sporadic damage across several states across the Midwest.

"Winter Joy"
"Some snow needs to be carefully removed before it turns to ice."

Winter Driving Tips

1) When you see a semi's antenna swinging wildly back and forth, it means it's heavy with ice and you need to be careful. If the ice is collecting on the antenna, it might also be coating the road.

2) If you suspect the road may be icy, watch the tires of the cars and trucks as they go past. If they're spitting up spray, you're on melted slush and not ice. If there's no spray behind the wheels, slow down or get off the road.

3) The best defense in a snowy, icy situation when you *have* to be out in it is to slow down. The faster you go, the less time your wheels are in contact with the road, meaning the less friction you have with the road. This is also true in spring thunderstorms.

4) On ice or snow-packed roads, the most dangerous time is going downhill. I say that because the evidence was apparent one day when I got back on the road. Most of the vehicles in the ditches and median were on the down-side of a hill. Slow down before the crest of the hill and leave plenty of room ahead of you. If a vehicle brakes and starts skidding, you'll have time to react cautiously instead of following it into the ditch.

5) If road conditions are questionable and there is a high wind, be aware of wind breaks like buildings, trees, and overpasses. If you are steering into the wind and the wind suddenly stops, your car can veer in the opposite direction onto the shoulder or into the other lane.

6) If you see a car in the ditch perpendicular to the highway, chances are it spun off the road in other words, the road is icy.

7) If you see one car in the ditch on its top, it might be a careless driver, but if you see several cars upside down, they were on sheer ice. I drove from Des Moines to Omaha the day after an ice storm and counted more than a dozen cars upside down. It was unreal.

"Ice Storm Remnant"
"Freezing rain has to be watched closely because it often turns to ice. The warmth of the engine began to free this ice from the mirror."

One Shot

Sometimes you only get one shot
I see beautiful pictures
Slide by my windows
With nowhere to stop
To get the perfect shot

Years ago my car stopped quickly
For a fiery red sunset
In Yellowstone, not recorded
My camera was not with me
I see it only in my memory

Each day my camera is with me
And I see shots I want
But 70 feet of semi can't stop
And soon the picture is gone
Or diminished to the ordinary

I would like to capture sights
But can't take careful aim
The few snapshots are poor
Often missing the intended sight
Or interrupted by CB and visor

The hurricane devastation
In Beaumont, Texas, and Mississippi
The swamps of Louisiana
The smoky Blue Ridge Mountains
Are best left to my memory

Roadway sunrises and sunsets
Are well worth recording
But the colors change rapidly
And stretch across the horizon
Impossible to capture, only enjoy

When I think of the pictures passed
I wonder about people I've missed
These strangers I see every day
How many times do I have one shot
To touch a life I'll never see again

I remember a driver
Who graciously let me to go first
I was chagrined later after
It took me a long time to dock
As I watched her flawless skill

A couple yelling at a patient clerk
Who remained calm with them
As she tried to help them out
Their behavior was embarrassing
For my new chosen profession

I apologized for their behavior
And complimented hers
She had the experience to know
The rude are a small number
"We all have a bad day sometimes."

2006

The Unnamed Rivers

Time after time, this rig has crossed over rivers
With no identity sign as to their names

It caused me to wonder why so many counties
Would not have pride to name their rivers

This concrete traveler is not privy to the names
Of rivers rushing below, carrying away the rains

Then one day I knew the answer to the puzzle
These weren't rivers, but creeks grown fat

The land is full of water; the creeks turned to rivers
The extra in every rain can only run into the creeks

The land I'm traveling has had more than its share
More than it needs, much more than it wants

Those digging out their homes, their soggy possessions
Have gone out to the curb, never to be seen again

Those who braced up houses with partial basements
Those who scrub and clean and scrub and bleach what's left

Those who thankfully have help, work side by side with family
With friends who give time to begin to restore a dwelling

Those who fight to reclaim their living space again
Have no use for rain today; only pray and hope for sun

2007

9
On the Road with God

> For consider your call, brethren; not many of you were
> wise according to worldly standards ... but God chose
> what is foolish in the world to shame the wise.
> —1 Corinthians 1:26a & 27

This is one of my favorite verses in the Bible. I was pretty naïve for most of my life. In some ways I still am. It caused me to look foolish to other kids in school sometimes. I fought it in college, but it turned to sarcasm, which I later had to rein in. After coming across that verse, I didn't worry so much about my foolishness. There were some who thought I was a fool for leaving a good teaching job, at a school I loved, to become a truck driver. Now, they didn't come right out and say that, but it was apparent from their questions and body language that at least in their own minds, and perhaps to other people, they called me a fool. But I have become a fool for the Lord's sake, because that foolish decision has given me time out in God's creation. I've been given time for thought, prayer, and contemplation, time to read, to write, and to ponder things God has put in front of me for my sake or for others.

Sometimes I just make foolish decisions. I left a warehouse in Wilton, Iowa, to deliver the rest of the load to Tipton, Iowa. Thunder and lightning started shortly before I left. As I was shutting my doors, lots of people were coming outside and looking at the sky. The man who unloaded me yelled at me to be careful of the coming storm. I had only 17 miles to go, so I thought I could beat it to Tipton. My only concern was that I was almost empty and the wind had been blowing out of the south all day. However, just as I got onto I-80, the highway dipped into a valley protected on the south by trees, which also hid the storm. I ran smack dab into it, and visibility went from a mile to 15 feet in seconds as we encountered a wall of heavy rain. Everyone was braking and putting on their flashers as they struggled to see. Cars and semis alike were pulling off the road. I slowed down with my flashers like the rest of them, but just kept focusing on the white lines to stay in my lane. A few of us kept moving through all the vehicles stopped on both shoulders. I knew from the weather radio that it was moving northeast and hoped to drive out of it. After three miles, it got lighter, and then I was at my exit. As I drove north to Tipton, I felt drained as I realized how much adrenalin I used getting through that scary situation. I also realized how foolish I had been to think I needed to race against a storm, instead of waiting a few more minutes to let it go on by. Trucking is often like life in that it is very fast-paced, with deadlines constantly looming over my head and pressure from myself and others always to try to do more. A fast pace can become dangerous when the perceived need to get down the road outweighs patience for things out of my control.

I read an article that said our society doesn't have room in it for boredom any more. Technology gives us opportunity to be in touch always. The down-side is we also don't have time to think, dream, imagine, or create, similar to how I felt when I was teaching. In trucking, the boring parts of driving, waiting to load or to unload, give me time to think and my imagination can be inspired. I remember well summer vacation growing up on the farm. When the chores were done, I was free to do pretty much what I wanted. Since we lived too far from town to walk to friends' houses, this meant finding ways to entertain myself at home. We didn't get a TV until I was in sixth grade. Reading was my favorite choice, and I could often be found laid out on the lawn all afternoon in the company of a good book. When the sunny spot where I started got too warm, I'd roll to the shade of a tree for a bit, until I got chilly and it was time to roll back. When I ran out of books, I moved on to reading my parent's collection of old Readers Digest magazines that dated back as far as World War II. I miss the days when life was less chaotic, and time spent in quiet pursuits alone like this was commonplace and seen as valuable.

In the truck, prayer is one of those quiet pursuits for which I now find ample time. In 2010, I was scheduling my home time around a class I was taking at my church, which meant I was rarely home for regular worship services. To help maintain my feeling of belonging with my congregation, I regularly borrowed the DVDs of recorded services to watch on the road. One week I watched a service, where a little boy was baptized, and I remembered he was born too early and had a condition that was almost fatal. It brought back memories of all the prayers I had prayed for him while my wheels were rolling. Perhaps because my daughter was pregnant, or just because I think babies deserve a chance, I prayed fervently. I cried through many of the prayers as I thought about someone so little having such a tough beginning. I wanted him to fight for his life. I had just read something that said we often do not pray big enough prayers, so I prayed big, sometimes talking as if the baby could hear me. When I saw him baptized, and how healthy he looked, the tears flowed. What a blessing!

Recently I had another occasion to pray for a little girl born with a hole in her diaphragm. She had a real tough time as the lower organs had found their way up into the chest cavity and crowded her lungs and heart. In the first three weeks of life she had endured four operations. I pray, cry and, yes, sometimes talk to her as if somehow the Spirit can convey my words. "I want you to fight! Fight for every breath. That's your job right now, breathe in … breathe out … breathe in … breathe out. I want you to live to feel the love your family has for you. They love you so much! Keep fighting, girl!" God is full of mystery and in dire need I'm willing to pray in a variety of ways, to pray the big prayer, to pray fervently, and even to appear foolish.

Out on the road I find it easy to talk to God. Most of the time it doesn't sound like a traditional prayer, but if prayer is talking to God, then I pray a lot as I am alone in the truck. I am allowed to drive up to eleven hours at a time before taking a ten-hour sleep break. I might pray for someone who's in need. I might pray for wisdom if I'm in an unfamiliar place or if the weather is threatening. Often I compliment God about the great sunrise or the beauty of the winter fog that turned the trees into a sparkling

Christmas card. Sometimes I laugh with Him, like the time I commented that the sunset would be subtle because of the cloud cover, only to be shocked a bit later at a gorgeous red sunset shining through a break in the clouds. It was as if He were saying, "I can do anything."

In southern Minnesota one April morning, I viewed a beautiful sunrise. I was driving east on I-90 as the clouds were turning pink, and then it got better as I approached the Mississippi and the pink was reflected through the slim, dark tree trunks in the flooded backwaters of the river as I crossed into Wisconsin. The next night I got to watch a wonderful moonrise as it struggled to free itself from low-lying clouds. Another day, I read a devotional written by a man who was looking forward to seeing "the pretty conjunction of the waning moon and the planet Mercury." My first thought was, who remembers when that happens? I wasn't even sure what he was talking about. Then later that night, I glanced over at the small crescent moon and right below it was a bright star. I always enjoy the moon and remembered what I had read and knew the star was Mercury.

Driving at night, especially on open highways, offers a unique perspective when my surroundings are hidden in the shadows with limited areas being illuminated by my truck and other vehicles. One night I was traveling from Missouri up to Iowa on I-35. I saw something fly toward me in my headlights. It was light in color, so I doubted it could be a bat. I didn't feel an impact, so I assumed it missed my truck. About a hundred miles later, I stopped to fuel up. As I walked around to put fuel in the passenger side tank, I saw a cecropia moth in the grille. Always looking for teachable moments for my granddaughters, I took it off the front of my truck. I was shocked when I felt its feet cling to my finger. It was still alive! The wings were a bit tattered on the edges, missing some of their velvet, and at least one wing was dislocated. I kept it on the dash, because it didn't make any moves to fly, and it eventually died. My daughter had a shadow box she hadn't used, and it was the perfect size in which to keep it. It reminds me of how strong God made the will to live in His creation. Whether it's a moth pinned against a semi, a tree growing out of rock I saw in Wyoming, a potted columbine I didn't have time to plant in the fall that grew on top of the ground in the spring, or a baby who is fighting for her life, the will to live results in some amazing things.

Semi Serious | 97

I think of my oldest granddaughter who reacted to my voice by kicking, while she was still in the womb. She was not only living, but was developing a relationship, an emotional attachment to her grandmother that I didn't even realize until I visited one day. I saw her starting to fuss in her baby swing, while my daughter tried to rest nearby just a little longer. I called out, "Hi, Hannah, it's Grandma!" She stopped fussing, looked at me and smiled the biggest smile. While I was enjoying the warmth in my heart from a smile meant for me, my daughter sat up and said, "Did you see that? Not only did she stop fussing, but she changed her whole attitude when she heard you!" Yes, she knew her name and she remembered I was someone she enjoyed. Before becoming a truck driver, I was able to see my granddaughter more often, but no matter how long between visits, it took only seconds for her to remember me when I called out the phrase she had heard many times before she was born.

I hadn't done much traveling in my life. There was a lot of the United States I hadn't seen. That's another thing this new career has added to my life, though the parts of the United States I see are not exactly tourist destinations. I do feel like I have gotten to know real people who live in other regions of the country. We are pretty much alike. All the personalities I see at home are the kinds I see on the road, too. We may like different foods, cheer for different teams, or speak with a different accent, but our similarities outnumber our differences. I particularly enjoy watching a smile spread across a woman's face as she notices the big rig passing by is driven by a woman. I got passed one day by a bright pink cab. Knowing it was a woman driver, I watched to catch her eye. We both had big smiles on our faces. One day I was buying some food and when asked if I wanted a drink, I told the young woman serving me I had some in my truck. She perked up, "You drive a truck?" When she found out I had been a teacher, she said, "Wow, that's quite a jump!" I told her most people are surprised it's less stressful than teaching.

My favorite safe place to be in the company of men is in the truckers lounge during a football playoff game. The cheering and teasing remind me of times watching with the men in my extended family. Recently I watched a game in a lounge where I was the only female, but it was ten minutes before I realized only two of us were white. During an exciting part when my team made a great play, I jumped out of my seat and yelled with the rest of them. It seemed like they just noticed I was there because I'd been pretty quiet. They began to include me in conversations. I encounter very little racism on the road, perhaps because we all have a job to do out here and encounter the same kinds of frustrations. Also, I spent five years teaching on the south side of Chicago from 1973 to 1978. Once on a bus ride back from downtown where the whole school had gone to the play, *Five on the Black Hand Side*, it was ten minutes before I noticed I was the only white person on the bus, and it seemed like the most natural ride. In fact, I was with a fellow teacher on the north side one day, going to a class. I was uncomfortable on the streets at first and then realized everyone was white. The quality of the school I taught at and the quality of the students and parents that I had contact with had made race irrelevant to me.

I don't always have to be out of my driver's seat to have encounters with other folks. A variety of people will gesture for me to sound my air horn. My general rules are the following: not in heavy traffic, not in town, and not for adults or teenagers. There are exceptions. I passed by a group of teenagers out "walking beans," and I knew they were probably hot, tired, and bored. They got what they wanted and waved back in appreciation. Years ago I helped supervise a group my son was in, who was raising money for a swing choir trip. For those not familiar with the term, walking beans means going out into a farmer's soybean field and attacking weeds that have resisted other attempts to kill them. Armed with hoes or small sickles, the teenagers earned the money for their swing choir trip in sweat and aching muscles. I gained an appreciation for my son's personality as he and the others joked, entertained, and encouraged each other in the hot summer sun.

An exception to the adult rule was one Fourth of July as an entire family was assembling chairs on their front lawn out in the country to enjoy the fireworks in a nearby town. The dad saw me coming and modeled the signal for my horn and had the youngsters all following his example. We all smiled and waved to each other as I pulled the cord and blasted the horn.

Although I'm a big believer in looking for the good in people and I truly enjoy the positive interactions I have with random folks on the road, I also know that I can't be foolish enough to trust that everyone I see has good intensions. As a solo woman driver, I do have to be alert to my surroundings. If I have to stay overnight in a city, I stay in my bunk with the curtain closed. There is safety in the fact that no one knows what kind of person is inside my truck. I might be a mean, six-foot-seven, burly guy who hates to be awakened. On only two occasions have I been scared of people. When I was a rookie, I was parked in a bad neighborhood in Chicago. The trucker next to me warned me to lock my trailer, which I did. But all night long, women would knock on my door looking for "work." I called a dear friend in Texas, and she talked to me and prayed with me until I was at peace. I slept well the rest of the night, even though the knocking continued.

The second occasion was in daylight in a bad part of Detroit, which I had been told was *not* a bad part of town. A total of six people begged money from me while I waited to get unloaded. Unfortunately for the last five, the first one was so assertive that I became afraid and I refused him. They had a variety of reasons for needing money, but I didn't know what they actually planned to do with it. I did talk to one of the security officers, but when he was there, they weren't around. Again, I called for prayer support. When I was safely down the road, I regretted not giving them one of the crosses I often give out. They might have kept them or sold them for enough money for a meal, but it didn't occur to me until later. Fear has a foolish way of clogging rational thought.

Other things bring fear to my mind. In my rookie year, I had to drive from a southern suburb in Chicago to a northern suburb and then back to another southern suburb. Driving that much in Chicago was exhausting and took up most of my day. I thought the warehouse fire just blocks before the shipper was the end of the day. Then I thought the flat tire, after I was loaded, was the end of the day. No, after the tire was fixed, I sat in my truck in the dark, in the shipper's lot, that was now completely deserted. I didn't know how to get back to the interstate, where I knew a place to sleep. That was a moment when I knew there was no one to lean on but God. I muttered a fearful prayer and headed out the gate with tears running down my face and fear in my heart. There in the distance was the answer to my prayer. With lights flashing, a few fire trucks were still on the scene. With my voice breaking, I asked for directions; four turns later I was on the interstate. I didn't even care it was full rush hour with some crazy drivers. I knew where I was and where I was going.

What is the antidote to foolishness? Truth. The truth is that God is here with us and active in our lives. Our culture may try to get rid of Him, keep Him out of schools, courthouses, public places, and even out of politics, but He's still here. It's not His nature to force people to believe in Him, and He is extremely patient. He wants us to come to Him willingly. He wants us to praise what He has done. He wants us to listen to Him to do things to help others. He wants us to love Him and show that love to others. He wants us to tell others what He has done for us.

While I was compiling this book, I found a couple of interesting things in the Bible about truth, one of which I hadn't remembered reading before. In John 18: 37–38, Pilate was talking to Jesus and asked, "So You are a king?" Jesus answered, "You say I am king." I remembered that part. But Jesus continues: "For this I was born, and for this I have come into the world, to bear witness to the truth. Everyone who is of the truth hears my voice." Nothing was said at that moment about forgiving, saving, or redeeming, which is also what He did. He didn't say, "One of the reasons I came into the world." He seemed to place a tremendous value on truth. In John 8: 31b–32, Jesus says, "If you continue in My word, you are truly My disciples, and you will know the truth and the truth will make you free."

After my second weekend at the School for Lay Ministry, I thought of a way I could work and be able to be home every night. Before I could do anything about the idea, I had a conversation with a fellow trucker quite unexpectedly that gave me reason to believe that my time on the road with God might not be finished yet. I delivered a load to a warehouse in Chicago that I had been to—and one that I like because it gives us plenty of room to maneuver. I was at the door waiting so I could give the paperwork. Another trucker came up and with a smile asked, "How's Chicago treating you?" Sometimes I don't feel that great being in the windy city, but this place was a favorite of mine and I told him so. I added I had taught at a high school on the south side in the 1970s. After this small comment, I felt as though he were more relaxed when talking to this white woman. The conversation went on from there until he began to ask questions. They started about church and religion, but then began to get into faith. Perhaps because I was just recently at the School for Lay Ministry, I quickly became aware that God put this man in front of me. We were from vastly different cultures, but he was full of questions. I said a silent prayer, "Lord, please don't let me mess this up." I didn't directly answer his questions, but we discussed them, as one person of faith to another.

Time and again he said, "Just one more question." The questions got deeper and deeper until he revealed a night of a spiritual battle between good and evil and he was somehow convinced to choose the good. Because he seemed to be an acute thinker, I asked him if he knew the word discernment. "Yes." I told him what I had learned over the weekend that we cannot discern for ourselves, but it is a gift from God. That seemed either to satisfy him or give him something to contemplate. We said good-bye and went back to our trucks, where I said a prayer of thanks and praise for God's help with the conversation. Maybe God still has reasons for me to be out here on the road, moving me to do things for Him, to be inspired by His creation, and most of all to stay close to Him in all situations.

Dear Lord, I am sometimes shocked at the things You nudge me to do out here among strangers. But I have learned that when I am convinced You are the one urging me to do something it is always the right thing to do. Thank You for these experiences. Forgive me for when I've missed the message or when I don't think I can contribute. You can use anything to make a difference. In Your will, amen.

View from My Windshield

The view from my windshield
As I haul a load down the road
Is why I am still trucking

It's not leaning into a dirty engine
To grab the oil dip-stick
Getting gloves and coat greasy

It's not sweeping out a dirty trailer
And having to be so careful
Not to miss a step climbing down

It's not the delays in getting loaded
It's not the uncertainty
Of where they'll send me next

It's not having to drive all night
When the oncoming lights blind me
And guarantee a headache

It's not driving on snow and ice
To get a load to its destination
Cautiously watching civilian drivers

It's not lying on the ground in the snow
Under the trailer with my hammer
To loosen frozen brake pads

It's not walking into a noisy warehouse
Watching out for speeding forklifts
To talk to someone out of patience that day

And it's certainly not using truck stop showers
That are small, bare, and cold
Mostly not filled with my things

The view out my windshield inspires
Appreciation for God's creation
And His ever-present part in it

The view out my windshield surprises
With unexpected glimpses of the wild
Whether large, small, walking or flying

The view out my windshield brings peace
As I have time to contemplate
My life, relationships, and my God

2010

Remembering History Lived

They talk of Dr. King today
Forty years since he was lost
Peace and freedom put on hold

A black man talks of loss
He talks of white applause
He talks about black sorrow

Wait—whites were happy?
I was saddened by it
Why was I different?

White girl shortly off the farm
Knew no American blacks
Only students from Africa

Slowly, I remember a professor
Spoke of his Freedom Rider friend
Who lost his life in the South

He asked us to walk downtown
Some yelled out "nigger lover"
Hatred from my own race

A hint of what it was like
Two years before Dr. King
Was lost to our generation

The words of a white man
Bobby broke the news to those
Waiting for him to speak

Semi Serious

His moving words to them
Spoken without any notes
Of coping with Jack's death

They knew he understood
Such a huge loss as this
No riots in their city

Jump forward two months
Bobby, whose hand I shook
His blue eyes forever dimmed

Yes, saddened that April
Like that June day later
Like September '63 earlier

Five years after Martin and Bobby
In a phone call conversation
With a future principal

"Our school is 95% black."
Silence followed—I said, "Yes?"
She gave opportunity for exit

I plunged ahead into the work
Learned a whole new culture
Grew confidence in myself

2008

She Knew Her Name

I know she knew her name
Weeks before she was born
She played games with Daddy
She knew her mama's songs
She even knew Grandma's call
She knew she was adored

Her mother was the first to feel
The moves of life within
She marveled at the love she felt
And expressed it singing
In time and patience
Others felt it and had to grin

Her daddy felt the moves and kicks
He played with the tiny life
Pressing back against the moves
Brought kicks of "baby out of sight"
They played "find Daddy's voice"
She was almost always right

Grandma lived close by
And heard about the games
She tried a few herself
Every time she came
Just for fun she called out
"Hi, Hannah! It's Grandma!"

There are some who would deny
The unborn can be a babe
They use the term fetus

As if not worthy to be named
This child within my daughter
Responded to her name

On a banner in a small church
By baptismal font: "You are mine
I have called you by name."
In the book of Jeremiah:
"Before I formed you in the womb
I knew you," said the Lord

I know she knew her name
Later I stopped by for a while
She was fussy in her baby swing
I walked in and bade her "Hi …"
My heart melted as my greeting
Turned a fuss into a smile

I know she knew her name
Weeks before she was born
She played games with Daddy
She knew her mama's songs
She even knew Grandma's call
She knew she was adored

2006

"Wisconsin Rays"
"I captured rays I didn't see. I was taking a picture
of the shadows in Plymouth, WI.
The total black and white of the scene
fascinated me. The rays were a gift."

"Angel Wings"
"There have been a few times when the wispy clouds look like angel wings..
They are often elusive to a camera lens."

"Western Plains Afternoon"
"Taking a quick break, I was struck by the rugged landscape and included the tree for interest.
The rays were a surprise!

10

The Cross Lady

*So I saw that there is nothing better than that a
man (woman) should enjoy his work.*
—Ecclesiastes 3:22

When my granddaughters were small, their mom wanted to do something to earn some income at home to help with the family budget. She researched online and found something she thought would work. She sent off for the materials and began making crosses with the intent of selling them or returning them to the company for a lower price. When I saw the finished product, I wanted one. It was made up of four horseshoe nails that had been bent and then put together with colored wire. The result were crosses in a wide variety of colors, with a lanyard of narrow leather tied in such a way that you could wear the cross at whatever length you wanted. I liked it because I could shorten it, so it would never interfere with the seat belt I wear during my workday. Thinking of a couple of friends, I bought a few more for them.

My daughter finished the first order of materials and ordered more while sending off the finished products to the company. Her husband got involved by putting the double bend, which required more strength, in half of the nails. He also built a finishing rack for her to hang the crosses on after they had been dipped in polyurethane, which made it a far less messy process. She was getting faster at the craft and was fashioning them anytime she was sitting. I pictured it as similar to people who knit on a regular basis while watching TV, visiting with someone, or even talking on the phone. Because she was getting faster, she ordered a third batch of materials and soon sent off the finished crosses from the second order. My mother's pride was showing as I heard about how she was doing, and I asked her to save me several crosses. My friends had loved the crosses, and I began to think of people in church who might be in need of a cross because of sickness or the loss of a loved one.

When I was a pastor's wife at our first church, I had started a prayer bear ministry with one little bear ornament. I gave it to a new widow near Christmas shortly after we moved to town. She wasn't home, so I left it with a note. When I didn't hear from her, I worried that I had offended my first parishioner, but when she saw me at church a few days later, she was delighted with the bear and the prayers. It blossomed quickly into more when I found some one-inch flocked bears in a craft shop. As I gave a white bear away, I kept a colored one for myself to remind me to pray for them. After a while I put a name on each bear to remind myself of the numerous people I prayed for. By the time we moved, I had given out over a hundred bears and had to rotate who I prayed for.

My daughter called me on the road one day upset, because most of her crosses were returned because of some minor detail that made them imperfect. Because she was already on her third batch of material, she was feeling defeated. Trying to encourage her in doing a craft I liked, I told her to save more for me in a variety of colors and I would buy them the next time I visited. Soon I became my daughter's best customer. People in the class I was taking at church all got to choose the colors they liked. I bought several crosses and took them on the road with me in case there might be someone who would like one. Initially, I thought I would sell some for her, and I did for a while.

The first time I had the urge to give a cross to a stranger, I was a little hesitant, but I soon found out that when I was moved to give a cross away, it was always well received. Sometimes it was just the encouragement someone needed. As the Spirit continued to prompt me, I gave more of them away. Sometimes I saw someone tired behind the counter of a fast-food restaurant or at a truck stop. Sometimes it was someone at a warehouse. Once in a while I leave a cross with the tip without mentioning it to my waiter or waitress. I walk out with a little smile on my face, kind of like leaving a May basket on someone's doorstep. Once in an Indiana truck stop, my waitress came running after me. I thought here was one person who didn't want a cross. Instead she said, "Come back, I have something for you." She gave me three CDs of testimony from her church. I didn't want to take all three, but she insisted. Her church tapes the testimonies from worship and makes copies to give away. I still have them and occasionally listen to them again.

One day, I texted my daughter to find out how many crosses she had made. By this time she had decided not to order any more materials, because despite all the changes she made, the crosses continued to be rejected. My intention was to buy her whole inventory, because I just kept finding more people who might like a cross. My daughter asked me why I wanted to know the number she had. When I told her, she couldn't believe me. I asked her again how many, and she said she was counting. My daughter and I have a unique relationship, which had its deep beginning when she was twenty years old and came home from college one weekend to apologize to me for how she acted when she was a teenager. Her friends at college gave her an objective view from the times they had met me and some things I had done or said, but it still came as a shock to me. I assured her that her teenage attitude was something every parent faced, and I didn't think she was an exception to the teenage angst. It did warm my heart, though. When it came to negotiating a price I should pay for the crosses, we did have quite a time disagreeing. Oh, not in the usual sense, she wanted me to pay less, and I wanted to pay her more. We ended up laughing and said, "Who does this?" and divided the difference.

My pastor periodically gets a bag of crosses to give away at her discretion. When I can, I help her out with the nursing home services. One Sunday, she called me over to a young woman in a wheelchair. As she gave the cross to her, she introduced me as "the cross lady" she had told her about. She gave me the cross to explain the meaning of the parts of the cross: the nails (used in Jesus' hands), the wire (symbolic of the thorns on His head), and the leather lanyard (symbolic of the whip laid across his back). As I took the cross out of the package and placed it around her neck, she cried. I gently rocked her chair and wiped her tears as the worship service started. Since then we have visited several times, and when I am tired or feeling sorry for myself, it only takes a visit with this young Christian lady, with so many limits in her life, to put my heart back into proper perspective.

In Kentucky, after a long night, I walked into a truck stop in the wee hours of the morning. A young man and woman working there were talking about a group that had been a little rude. They were disappointed in them, because it was a Christian group. I offered each of them a cross and they quickly forgot about the group and focused on which color they wanted. When I went into the restaurant to have breakfast, the young man was my waiter. As I looked over the menu, he pulled up a chair and waited for my order. I was his only customer. He explained his feet hurt from his new boots. He put in my order and came back to my table to talk some more. He had graduated from a police academy and wanted to work on a drug task force, but realized soon he would be an old man before he got that job. I told him I had been a teacher before I began trucking and talked about my philosophy: teach students to think and to have high expectations of themselves. He said he'd been in an accelerated math class in high school, was the best in his calculus class, and helped other students so well, his teacher allowed him to circulate around the classroom answering questions. He seemed ready to talk about his options. We covered a number of subjects as I had breakfast. When it was time for me to go, he mentioned he might go back to school and become a high school math teacher. As I was going to sleep, I reflected on that conversation. I couldn't remember having such an in-depth conversation with a stranger. Part of it was because I knew he was a man of character when he told me he was the line cook, but had volunteered when one of the waitresses quit. That's how he got the blisters on his heels, walking in inappropriate footwear. I didn't even piece together the parts of the conversation about teaching, calculus, and his final statement about going back to school until later. The only advice I gave him was on taking care of his blisters. Part of me felt I was there at the right time to be a sounding board as he thought about the path he might take next. Listening is so important.

I asked a waiter another day if he'd like a cross and asked him to relay a message to the woman making omelets at the buffet if she'd like one. They both chose a cross and I began packing up the crosses. As I was putting on my coat, the trucker at the next table said, "That will come back to you ten-fold." I asked him if he'd like a cross. He pulled out his billfold and took out a five dollar bill. I told him I gave them away. He took out another five dollar bill. I asked him what he was doing. He took out a third five and said, "It's Christmas, and I want three of them." I laid out the crosses and as he chose, he told me his story. He hit bottom and finally came to believe in Christ and was now a trucker and making it with the help of God. It was a wonderful, unexpected testimony I felt privileged to hear.

One winter day after a horrendous snowstorm, I got stuck and shoveled out all eight drive tires to get going. The next day I was five hundred miles away in a truck stop and got stuck again in snow from the same storm. This time I got some help in the way of a small jeep with a snow scoop on the front. The driver told me he was just doing it to help out the drivers, so they could get parked. Another trucker came over later and took the shovel from me and finished digging out my tires and told me, "Now when you go forward, keep going so he can come behind you and clear the rest of this snow."

When the snow was moved, I parked my truck, changed into dry clothes, put on my good coat to go in and have a hot meal. I saw the jeep was still at work, so I grabbed a small baggie of crosses and flagged the driver down. He seemed confused when I thanked him and I was thinking he had a real short memory as I reminded him of who I was. Then he brightened and said, "I didn't recognize you. You clean up real good!"

I laughed and said, "It's probably the smile that wasn't there when I was stuck." He chose a cross for his little girl, and I told him to pick one for himself too. As he was deciding on colors, I said, "I am just so thankful for your help. I got stuck yesterday and no one stopped to help as I shoveled out twice as many tires."

One warmer day at a warehouse after dropping my empty trailer, I was waiting at the window for an unusually long time for the clerk to let me know if my load was ready. Trying to be patient, I didn't interrupt her as she worked with papers. Four other truckers came in, signed in, and sat on chairs provided while waiting their turn. Finally, after ten minutes, the woman at the window spoke, "I'll be with you in a minute." After

Semi Serious | 115

ten minutes, that's all she said! I turned around and caught the eye of the trucker behind me and mouthed, "Wow!" She chuckled, and we made some small talk as I continued to wait. Eventually I got out of there and was able to hook up to the loaded trailer. Later, when I weighed my load at the nearest truck stop I met the trucker again. She flagged me down and asked if I was headed down the road or staying the night. She wanted to have supper with me. She told me, "When you turned around and mouthed the word *wow*, I just knew I had to get to know you better!" I'm very cautious with male truckers, but I decided it might be fun to have supper with a fellow female trucker. It was great conversation, and we exchanged cell phone numbers and truck numbers. She has trucked for over thirty years and was a great source of information when I was unsure of something minor and didn't feel like calling dispatch.

In Chicago one warm spring day, I noticed several men with shopping carts going up and down the street. They all seemed to be bringing scrap metal of various kinds to a recycling place a half block away. Though they appeared to be poor, there were no disagreements, and in fact, I saw a couple of men help others, directing them where to go or helping them separate non valuable trash from the metal. As I waited, I heard a small bell and looked up to see a man pushing a small cart. He stopped by the docks, and I could clearly see the pictures of ice cream treats. Always willing to contribute to someone trying to make a living by selling a good product, I got out and made a purchase. His English wasn't very good, but we communicated well enough for me to enjoy a cool dessert. After he left, I thought I could have given him a cross, but it was too late. When I pulled out of the dock and parked to close the trailer doors, a man and woman walked past with a shopping cart. Perhaps I could give the woman a cross. I chose a purple cross to go with her outfit and walked over to give it to her. She was delighted as she explained that she had just had cataract surgery and had to wear dark glasses. As we talked, the man came back and she showed him the cross. He answered in another language. I asked if he would like a cross. She translated, and I went back to the truck for it. When I came back, we continued to talk about some of their struggles and they were very curious about a single woman driving a big truck around the country. We also talked about faith, and I walked away feeling enriched by the conversation with two people who had very little, but seemed content with life.

In Hopkins, Minnesota, I had a very pleasant conversation once with a woman at a receiving office. We covered several subjects, including our faith and what we believed about the Holy Spirit. It was a conversation I might have had with a member of my church—and I was in a warehouse! When I was unloaded, I went back to the office to get my paperwork, but she was busy with a line of truckers. I got my paperwork from the lumper (a person who gets paid to unload the trailer). I pulled out, closed the doors, and headed for the guard shack at the entrance. As I parked my truck to finish up my sleep break, I felt the urge to give this woman a cross. Why didn't I think of that while I was inside the warehouse property? The urge to give her a cross was strong, but I knew that with the stricter regulations after 9/11, the guard wouldn't let me back in the lot. The urge was still there. Lying wasn't an option, so what would I say to the guard? Still the urge was there. Finally I said to God, "Okay, but I know I'll just be circling back to this parking space." So I drove out of the lot and back to the guard house. Looking at the guard, I said, "I forgot to give something to the woman in the receiving office." The guard looked at me and then started writing on her clip board.

She handed it to me for my signature and said, "I put down that you forgot your paperwork." Then she let me back in. I couldn't believe it! That just does not happen when there is a guard on duty. Marveling at how God works when He wants something done, I drove to the receiving office shaking my head and grinning. I brought in several colors of crosses for the woman to choose. I intended to give her a cross, but she was so excited about them, she invited the lumper over to get one too. I was caught off guard, and when he asked how much, I told him $5. He bought two of them and wore both of them with a big smile on his face. The woman paid for hers and I felt bad, but I didn't want to accept money from the man and give her a free one. That money went into the collection plate later. The woman was glad to see me to tell me how much she had enjoyed our conversation. She was sorry she was so busy when I left. I told her I felt the same way about our conversation. She is someone I wish I could see again, but she works weekends, and I have only been there on weekdays since.

I was in northern Missouri when I got dispatched to a warehouse in Joplin. By this time, I had bought all of my daughter's crosses, because giving them away was fulfilling and just way too fun. I immediately counted how many crosses I had with me to give out in Joplin. A search of my truck turned up only seventeen crosses. Many times I have as many as thirty-five or forty, but I was too far from home to change the amount I had. I parked my truck first and checked in. Then I went back in later with my pathetic number of crosses and I talked to one of the three women in the office. After showing her the bag of crosses I quickly told her my daughter made them and I give them away, so she wouldn't think I was trying to sell something. She opened the bag and started counting them right away and then said, "There's enough. We have fourteen people who lost their homes." I went back to my truck. I wasn't sure who the fourteen people were and hadn't thought to ask. It wasn't a very big number given the devastation the city had been dealt. The warehouse was on the north end of town, and I saw no damage in the area. I fell asleep in the bunk and woke up wondering if my truck had been called to a dock. I went in to check and was waiting behind another trucker. When he left, the woman who took the crosses suddenly announced loudly, "Ladies, this is the woman who gave me the crosses." Then turning to me she said, "Both these women lost their homes in the tornado." The women jumped up and were on their way over to give me a hug. With tears in their eyes, they thanked me profusely. I was stunned at the impact of those two crosses. Back in my truck, I realized what I thought was an inadequate number of crosses was more than enough for God to use to start healing people in just that one company.

On January 12, 2012, I thought this book was finished. I stopped to fuel my semi in Tomah, Wisconsin, after driving through that state's first snow of the season. While I was inside the truck stop, I overheard part of a conversation of a young woman on a cell phone. She had just received news that a member of her family was in the hospital. I sensed she and her parents needed a cross. My semi was in front of the fuel pumps, but I quickly found the bag of crosses and grabbed three. She was just walking toward her car, so I ran through the snow to catch her. I quickly pulled the crosses out of my pocket and said, "My daughter makes these, and I give them away. I overheard part of your conversation, and I have one for you, your dad, and your mom." She took the crosses, gave me a hug, and thanked me as tears began to run down her cheeks. As I got in the truck and realized I still had my dirty work coat on, I hoped it hadn't gotten her coat dirty. As I drove on down the road, I prayed for her family. I was glad to have listened to the prompting and hoped she didn't feel quite as alone with the news she had just gotten. The road conditions were not ideal for an emotional driver. The snow had left me tired, and I hoped to at least get into Minnesota before I parked. Instead of feeling tired, I felt energized from the brief encounter, and I got 160 miles into Minnesota before parking for the night. The way God shows up to tweak this cross ministry is absolutely remarkable. His ways are ever new and exciting, but I am humbled to play a small a part in them.

Lord, You amaze me with how well You know my circumstances and the people I encounter out on the road. I have never conversed with so many strangers in my life. They are not strangers to You, as I have witnessed the impact these crosses have had on them. There have been so many people who have received crosses, and I can't tell You the names of more than a dozen or so. But I don't have to know their names, because You know everything about them. You love them enough to use a trucker to bless their day. Thank You for letting me be a part of this unique ministry of Yours, amen.

The Big Picture

In my truck, I'm up higher
Giving me a big view of the road
To be safe, I need the big picture
Of ditches, crossroads, and vehicles

Potential hazard is the official term.
When I see one up ahead
I need to quickly plan my move
Keeping those around me safe

My dad coached me about my 4-H pig
When it was small we practiced
He said, "Never let it get by you now
And when it's older it won't try."

One of our neighbors got a baby pig
He let it sit and cuddle in his lap
I warned him one day she'll be 300 lbs.
He didn't see the big picture.

When my children were very young
I heard someone give wise advice
"When a 2 year-old shows his temper
Imagine him as fifteen years old."

Poor behavior is better addressed
At age two than at age fifteen
Some parents placate, not address
They don't see the big picture

When I went for my master's degree
Credit applications were in every bag
With each bookstore purchase
I cringed at this student temptation

I started to teach my kids about credit
Years later it was a big news story
College kids with huge credit debts
They didn't see the big picture

There are people who don't believe
In God the Creator, Son, and Spirit
It's a myth or a foolish belief
And their lives fill with other things

I know God is very real in my life
He has protected me, chastised me
Comforted me, and challenged me
To show Himself to those around me

At times I hear myself argue with Him
But He always wins and I follow
When I do what He urges me to do
It allows Him to show the big picture

2007

"Prayers for Peggy"
"This dream catcher was a gift from Peggy. It hung in
my truck to remind me to pray for her.
It continues to hang in that same place in memory of her."

11
Real Words

Likewise, the Spirit helps us in our weakness; for we do
not know how to pray as we ought, but the Spirit Himself
speaks for us with sighs too deep for words.
—Romans 8:26

Let us run with perseverance the race that is set before us,
looking to Jesus, the pioneer and perfecter of our faith.
—Hebrews 12:1b–2a

A prayer from my journal on December 31, 2009: "Thank You for my growth this past year. I trust You will help me grow even more in Your way in this coming year. Strengthen my weaknesses, temper my pride, expand my love of people, and fortify my will to walk in Your way. In Your gracious love, C."

Little did I know in what ways God would answer that prayer in 2010 and 2011. The day after Thanksgiving in 2010, I was driving from northwest Iowa to Winona, Minnesota, where my son and daughter were following a "shop till I drop" tradition they started. I hadn't had much sleep but wanted to join them, if not for shopping, for their company. I napped several times on the way. The last nap was longer, and I had a dream. Three men were talking to me. The first two were very complimentary (I wish I could remember what they said), and then the third man said, "You know what that means, don't you? You need to go to seminary." I was driving down the road and thinking about what the third man said but not knowing how I could possibly afford it. After about a half hour of thought, I suddenly realized the man had been in a dream. It was so real; it took that long to realize it was a dream. That is not to say I entirely dismissed the idea. It is still on my mind.

In the introduction I mentioned some extraordinary circumstances. One such incident was on a street full of warehouses in Wheeling, Illinois. Big trucks lined both sides of the street. I parked on the left side of the street near my docks and waited. When they called with the dock number, I got out to open the trailer doors. As I was opening the right door, I heard the words "Don't follow the door around." I stopped and peeked around the door just as a semi truck came roaring by. Those words saved me from certain injury. I have no doubt God quietly spoke the words that would strike me as unusual and cause me to stop and look. Someone asked me if there was someone behind me who could have said that. No, it was very quietly spoken. Besides, a driver would have yelled something like, "Look out! A semi's coming!!" As I thought about it later, I realized a person's warning would have been too late, because he or she wouldn't have known I wasn't going to look. It takes only a few seconds after the door is unlatched to move it around to secure it open. I heard the words just after the door was unlatched. The semi passed within two feet and was doing at least twenty miles per hour. It would have only taken a corner of his fender to hit the door hard enough to send me sprawling with whatever injury resulted from door or paving. Five words with a quiet warning, but with tremendous significance to this thankful woman!

For a while I blamed myself for being so careless. Then I realized when I'm parked on the right side of the street, I open the door without worry, because there's nothing but curb and grass there. The door doesn't even reach the sidewalk to take out a pedestrian. It is on one hand very humbling to know God was watching at that second and warned me. On the other hand, I want to tell everyone, "Look what He did!" As inept as I am at some things, He cared enough to speak in a way to stop me from injury. Since that incident, I check for anything near either door.

At times I get an urge to do something: call someone, share a poem, or write a note to someone. These are the ordinary, common things. Once in a while I get the urge to do something I wouldn't think of doing. One night as I drove east in Kentucky, I felt the urge to stop at a Cannonsburg truck stop to send an e-mail to my pastor about missing Bible study. I knew I didn't have time because I had to get to Virginia for a morning delivery. The thought wouldn't go away no matter what argument I came up with. If I stopped I'd have to change my log book, which I don't like to do. I'd have to short myself on sleep. Never a good idea. Whenever I argue with myself and find I am losing, I realize I am arguing with God. So I said, "Okay, if the scale I go by doesn't beep at me—which would record the time I go by—I will stop." Well, it didn't beep, so I stopped for a quick e-mail. As I was packing up my laptop, the woman at the computer table behind me spoke. Thinking she was making small talk, I replied, but her next sentence indicated I had misunderstood what she meant. She spoke one sentence at a time, and I misunderstood every one of them! When she finally stated her problem, she had her coat on and was leaving. As I comprehended what she had just shared with me, she turned back and said, "God bless you." I didn't think I did anything, but I knew she was in a spiritual battle.

I prayed for her all the way to my truck. I had to get some rest and just prayed myself to sleep. After a short night, I got up to get breakfast. I reached into a bag of crosses and took one out for her at random. She was at the same table, but was asleep. I quietly put the cross on the table and went to the restaurant, which was closed. Back at the truck, I felt the urge to write a letter to give her some hope. I knew nothing specific about her situation, but the letter flowed out of my pen—no rough draft. I decided to include the ten-dollar bill I was going to spend on breakfast. I never give cash to strangers. I also felt as though I should sign my name. I never give out my name on the road. The urge to sign was strong, as if it might say to her that I believed what I had written. She wasn't there, but her bag was, so I left the envelope on the table: "From the computer lady."

A week later, I was driving west in northern Illinois heading home to Iowa. The sun was out, and I was excited to be able to get to Bible study. As I crossed into Iowa, it began to snow big wet flakes. Disappointment came in a torrent of emotion—not again! Before I could feel too sorry for myself, I heard, "Missing last week's class had nothing to do with you." I thought back and realized the whole trip to Virginia was so God could put me where He needed me to sit, literally, so He could help that woman move back to Him. Through tears, I asked His forgiveness for being so blind. I also felt such a peace about her. I realized I would gladly do it again. I knew God loved her and was going to be there for her. I even wondered if perhaps He needed a writer, so the woman could read and reread the letter or even share it with a pastor or trusted friend. Sometime later I ran across 2 Corinthians 10:10, where the apostle Paul writes about himself: "For they say, 'His letters are weighty and strong, but his bodily presence is weak, and his speech of no account.'" I'm not a good verbal witness, but God sometimes speaks through my pen.

During another incident I felt I had made a foolish decision, and it turned out I was where God wanted me to be. It was Bible camp Sunday. I had talked a bit at the Saturday night service about my experiences. My favorite camp was a ranch in the Black Hills, so I wore a cowboy hat. I had planned to wear it Sunday morning when our committee served breakfast, but forgot it at home. I accepted my forgetfulness, until one of the cooks said, "We have ten minutes until we have to stir the eggs." Everything else was ready, and I thought, *Five minutes home, grab the hat, and five minutes back to church.* It seemed like a foolish thing, so I didn't tell anyone and just took off. I saw some bills on the pickup seat, so after I grabbed my hat, I swung by a mailbox. As I was rolling down the window, I saw a man crawling up the sidewalk to a building that was closed on Sunday. By the time I mailed the bills, he had tried to pull himself up by the door handle.

I parked my pickup and got out to see if he needed help. Together we decided to call 911, because he was afraid he might have broken his hip. When the EMTs came, they asked him how long he had been there. He thought fifteen to twenty minutes. She said, "Oh my, that's a long time in this cold." I left to get back to church, but her comment bothered me as I thought about how close I came not to going back for that silly hat. I began to cry. Part of me understood God wanted me to be there, but how long would it have been before he got help, if any at all? The responsibility weighed heavy on me, and I couldn't stop crying even as I parked at church. One of the church leaders gave me a hug and some good advice.

She said after I was done with my responsibilities for the breakfast, I should go over to the hospital and check on him. When I did, I found out that he had, indeed, broken his hip, and the EMTs were taking him via ambulance to another hospital.

That night, I was trying to get to sleep in my truck to start a trip early in the morning. I was having trouble because the events of the morning kept running through my head and what would have happened if I hadn't been there. With my head on the pillow and my eyes aching from the tears of the day, I heard a quiet voice say, "I would have sent someone else." Of course. I was so grateful that God cared enough to calm my spirit, and I fell into a peaceful sleep.

On a day with warm air, sunshine, and a continuous movie of His creation going by my windshield, I don't run out of things to thank Him for. Also within that solitude, I have been hearing and sensing from Him that I should do more for Him. I enrolled in the School for Lay Ministry and began in the fall of 2011. It is a commitment of four weekends a year for three years with a paper due each weekend. At the end of that time I should be able to determine what God is calling me to do. It may be writing or some other form of ministry such as preaching, visiting the ill and elderly, or possibly even attending seminary. Seminary seems foolish at my age, but one thing I have learned in the last two years is this: what we think is foolish may just be exactly what God wants. Something as foolish as going back home for my cowboy hat on Bible camp Sunday and found me helping a ninety-three-year-old man who had broken his hip in twenty-five-degree weather. Foolish became humbling.

One of the books for the School for Lay Ministry explained spiritual practices that will open me up to better hear what God wants. The chapter on discernment was particularly helpful. I was not familiar with the word until my pastor used it in a prayer for me. What I learned from the book is that I can't force discernment. It is a gift only God can give. I have to stay connected to God and be open to what He wants in whatever decision I might want to make. God communicates through the Holy Spirit and I need to be aware and listening. I did most of the practices as I drove down the interstate. One practice that surprised me was the chapter on self-evaluation, because I've done it many times in my life. I wrote out some notes on an index card. The first note said, "Silence— be still." I said it out loud and enjoyed several miles down the road. Then I decided I'd look at the next note: "Know how much God loves me." I know God loves me, but I thought about it anyway. I started to feel my heart. It was as if God were filling it up. It felt bigger and bigger until I didn't think it would fit in my chest. By this time I was wiping tears from my eyes as I realized I *didn't* know how much He loved me.

After talking to dispatch with news that my next trailer wasn't loaded, I resigned myself and made plans to try to sleep. Then I got the call—the load was ready! If I could go from the eastern edge of Iowa to the southeast corner of South Dakota, back to Storm Lake, Iowa, and on home to Webster City, Iowa, in the ten hours I had left, I could make it to worship Sunday. With the poor sleep I'd gotten, it didn't seem possible. I drove figuring I'd get as far as I could, but I was alert and I asked the same question several times, "Are we going to do this?" When I parked my truck at home by 2:30 a.m., I set my alarm for 8 a.m. and slept soundly. I figured God had a reason for me to be at worship. It was a good service. There was an event in the afternoon that sounded good, and I decided to go. Before the program started, my pastor introduced me to another pastor in the area, who asked if I would like to preach for a Sunday she would be gone. I realized that was the reason God wanted me to get home. Though I hadn't preached, I had given talks on retreats, and He would lead me through it.

Sometimes communication with God is unspoken. At the end of November 2011, I was in my car heading back to work 150 miles away. I started out about midnight, and by 3 a.m. I was getting tired both from driving in the dark and also fighting a strong wind. When I was thirty-five miles from work, I pulled over and took a short fifteen-minute nap. It was not long enough. Five miles from work I woke with a start and overcorrected. I struggled to bring my car to the middle of the road, but after three over-corrections, I saw the brown grass of the ditch. I thought, *This is it.* Whatever *it* was, I accepted it. The car was no longer under my control. My glasses flew off first thing, so I couldn't see what was going on. By the loud creaking, crunching, and moaning, I knew my car was being badly damaged. It seemed to last forever, but I'm sure it was over in a matter of seconds. I searched for my glasses but couldn't find them. I called the night dispatch, and she gave me numbers to call. I tried to open my door, but it opened only about ten inches. The molding around the seat belt anchor was broken, but the anchor held. I had a small cut on my little finger, but other than some bruises, I wasn't hurt.

A sheriff's deputy came, and we waited for a tow truck. He looked for my glasses but couldn't find them. After I got my computer and purse out of the car, the deputy took me to my company, where the truckers lounge had a couch to nap on. The dispatcher had taken my semi to go get my load, so I didn't have access to my spare glasses for about three hours. When she got back, I got them and took the company's courtesy car to go to my car to get the rest of my things for the week. I couldn't find it at the repair shop, so I drove to the scene of the accident. I had gone off the road equal distance between two telephone poles. I landed in a plowed field—one of the few fields without a fence—and missed someone's mailbox. When I was able to see the car, the repairman questioned my statement that I hadn't rolled the car. He showed me the damage and explained some of it had to have been the result of great force. For me the most convincing evidence was the brown grass sticking out of what was left of both side mirrors. He couldn't believe I didn't know I rolled it, but my eyes are so bad, I couldn't see a thing. And my glasses? They were neatly folded on the floor of the back seat, with nothing on them. Again I realized how amazing it was that I only suffered a quarter-inch cut and bruises. I let my pastor know, and she and her husband later met me to gives hugs and hear more of what happened.

I didn't know how to tell my children. Even though they are adults, it's not an easy thing to hear over the phone or in a text. Then I remembered their father was visiting my daughter on Thanksgiving weekend. I called his cell phone and told him to move to where they couldn't hear our conversation. My daughter told me later that was exactly the right thing to do. Meanwhile, I had started on the trip I had been dispatched on. Because I was heading her direction, we made arrangements to meet her and my son at a truck stop. They just needed to see me for themselves, and I was glad to get their hugs.

Later down the road, I recalled my last thought going into the ditch. I

Semi Serious | 129

know I didn't speak it aloud, and it wasn't even a prayer. It was a complete acceptance of whatever was about to happen. Throughout the whole crash, and even afterward talking to the deputy and tow driver, I was calm. Looking back, after seeing my totaled car and what it went through, I have no doubt that God heard my thought, took care of me, and even gave me the peace when I didn't ask for anything.

I drove my semi over three hundred miles the same day. I was glad dispatch put me back in the truck. It was a normal work week with just a few moments of anxious feelings. Though I didn't remember what direction my car drifted when I nodded off, my body did. Any time the truck got close to the right shoulder, I felt fear in my stomach and I forced myself to focus on slowly moving it to the center of the lane. During the week, I called the used car dealer where I bought the car. He had just put a newer year of the same model on his lot and promised to hold it until I got back. Coincidently, my mother had just given me a check a few days before, which together with the insurance settlement covered the cost of the replacement car. At home a week later, I got checked out at four doctors and bought a car. God had provided—even a cancelled dental appointment so I could have a cracked tooth repaired.

During the Saturday worship service, where I am liturgist whenever I am in town, my pastor mentioned the accident. She said I might at some point testify about it. As I read the responsive reading, based on Isaiah 40, one phrase caught my attention: "All people are fragile like the grass that withers and fades," and I could again see the brown grass through the windshield from that night. I spoke then to the congregation about that sight as the last thing I saw before my glasses flew off. I am very nearsighted, and it was probably a blessing that I didn't see what was happening. I told them about it briefly and how the seat belt held me so tight I didn't even know I'd been upside down. As my pastor talked about the peace Advent candle for that night, she mentioned the peace I had felt. As she spoke, there was a sacredness more clearly revealed to me about my experience. I understood then that my thought *This is it* was a complete surrender, and sometimes that's when God steps in. I can't help but feel the need to live a more faithful life in appreciation for more time to do so.

These are extraordinary circumstances, but I want to be clear about this: I am *not* an extraordinary person. Of the times I have had an urge to do something, or have heard words clearly spoken, I have not asked for them. It was nothing I did. The first time I heard clearly spoken words, it was a quiet reprimand. I was upset because I felt no one was listening to me. I was throwing rocks at a cliff in an old stone quarry and yelling. When I got hoarse and my arm was tired, I sat down on a big rock and then heard the soft words, "You need to listen." Not what I wanted to hear! It set me off again with the yelling and the rocks, but my body was spent and I sat down again. I heard it again: "You need to listen." This time I promised to listen for ten days. I sat on the rock for a while as I noticed the beauty around me. It was a moonlit night, there were trees nearby and the Mississippi River flowed serenely along. Through the next ten days, several references to listening appeared during my devotions. The last one was Mark 9:7: "This is my beloved son, listen to him!" I decided to make it my Lenten discipline. I found out I wasn't a good listener. That was thirty years ago. When I hear a quiet voice I think of God, but I think it is Jesus' Holy Spirit. My dad, who was very knowledgeable about all things created, referred to God as the Creator, so my first thought when I am outside, whether in my garden or an abandoned stone quarry, is of God, the Creator.

I have often wondered why Jesus, through the Holy Spirit, has spoken to me on a half dozen occasions. Sometimes I think it's because I'm so dense, He has to be obvious. But when I think back to the similarities of those occasions, the one common denominator is silence. Throughout my career in trucking, silence has been plentiful: a silence that comes even with the noise of the truck motor, the silence of being alone for long hours at a time, the silence of quiet prayer, the silence of reading the Word of God, the silence some would call loneliness, the silence I call solitude. Perhaps He has tried to talk to me at other times, but I haven't heard because of noise around me: the noise of people nearby, whether family, co-workers, strangers, or even people in church; the noise of TV or radio; the noise of a to-do list or a paperwork deadline at school; the noise of complete exhaustion, after a long, hard week of trucking. Though I am at the age of retirement, I am hesitant to retire because of all I have learned in the silence. But there will come a time when I will need to retire. If I want to stay in communication with Jesus, I will need to make time for silence.

Dear Lord, this has been Your book from the beginning, and I pray I have given everything You wanted me to put in it. Thank You for the times You have allowed my pen to flow with the words I couldn't speak. It has been an amazing journey, and I trust it will not be the last journey You take me on in this life, until it is time for my final journey. I am humbled by the love and care You have shown to me, sometimes in spite of my inconsistent connection to You. In Your grace, amen.

Fear and Trust

I fear God—not in the lightning bolt sense
Fear in the wow/awe kind of way
The strength of the storms of His creation
The falling star I was meant to see
The power to put satan in his place

I trust God—not in the "no harm will come" sense
Trust in the quiet thought of someone else
In a prayer of two people in His name
In a calmness of a decision in His will
In an urgent awareness of danger

I love God—not in the popular love song sense
Love because of the comfort He gives
Of timely words to impart needed wisdom
Of the warmth of His healing touch
Of the joy of newborn life

I know God—not in an omnipotent sense
Know that He exists then, now, and ahead
The longer I live, the more I know Him
But I know enough to know I don't know
All of what God is and does

2009

CPSIA information can be obtained at www.ICGtesting.com
Printed in the USA
LVOW050022250313

325779LV00001B/3/P

9 781449 775629